THE GREAT AMERICAN RESCUE MISSION™

Published by Dunham Books
6111 W. Plano Pkwy., Suite 2700
Plano, TX 75093
www.dunhamandcompany.com

Printed in the United States of America

This book is dedicated to the unseen heroes who are on the front lines of the Great American Rescue Mission, obeying God's command and investing daily into the lives of the fatherless.

May the Lord strengthen and fortify your resolve as you provide a guiding hand and a loving heart to the lost and hurting.

Acknowledgements

In loving gratitude to my Mom, for her strength and for sharing Jesus with me. To my uncle Bucky, thank you for being one of the few men who made an effort to stand up in my young life. My appreciation to other men and coaches who helped shepherd and guide me. And blessings on high to the wife of my youth, Tracey Smithbaker, and my children Madeline, Spencer, and Meredith; who have shared me in this mission and are committed to the cause.

FAITH • FATHERHOOD • FORGIVENESS

DEFEND THE CAUSE OF THE FATHERLESS...

ISAIAH 1:17

The family is God's chosen institution. Before communities and before the country, the family defines how we can live in health, and harmony and truth.

The breakdown of the family is directly assaulting the very principles of this Constitutional Republic. It is destroying the American ideal.

Our perfect union is collapsing…
Justice is compromised…
Domestic tranquility is broken…
Common defense is weakened…
The system of general welfare is broken…
And we are giving away Liberty and our children's future.

But God made you and I for a time like this.

America and her family are pleading to be rescued. She is worth preserving and defending.

"He left the ninety-nine for the one..."

Illustration by Rumaldo Holguin

Matthew 18:12

IN GOD we trust

"We the People of the United States, in Order to form a more perfect Union, establish Justice, insure domestic Tranquility, provide for the common defense, promote the general Welfare, and secure the Blessings of Liberty to ourselves and our Posterity, do ordain and establish this Constitution for the United States of America."

TABLE OF CONTENTS

★ ★ ★ ★ ★ ★ ★

"Freedom is never more than one generation away from extinction. We didn't pass it to our children in the bloodstream. It must be fought for, protected, and handed on for them to do the same."

— Ronald Reagan

CHAPTER ONE

A Broken Boy,
A Broken Family,
A Broken Nation

"THIS IS AN UNBELIEVABLY SOBERING TIME."

America's ability to be the shining city on the hill teeters tragically on a tipping point and is further compromised every day. Our resolve to be a global example of Christ's love is being tested. What we do next will determine the very identity of our beloved nation and its people.

Fatherlessness is tearing at the fabric of our country. It is the #1 societal issue that is decimating the family in America. Satan knows what he is doing.

The days of the mission field only being somewhere off in a distant land - are over. The days when we'd simply write checks and then, on the way to the post office, step over the carnage all around us - are over. Let us rise to the challenge and face the problems and brokenness in our own communities, and in our own country.

But be encouraged! God knows what He is doing and shares with us how to combat Satan's schemes. We must only listen to His heart and follow the instructions He so clearly provides - over 100 times in the Bible!

The issue is solvable and right before us – directly within the reach and responsibility of the local Christian church by intentionally and proactively "Defending the cause of the Fatherless…" Isaiah 1:17.

Fathers in the Field: Taking On the Culture Battle

We are coming to you out of a ministry position of **strength**, not out of weakness or distress. By listening to God's heart, faithfully following His mandate, and using His biblical model of rescue, we have built a successful and field-proven biblical ministry solution to forcefully push back against our broken culture.

We are aggressively taking on the battle in our neighborhoods, in our communities, and for our nation. Let's face it - we are fighting for our lives and relevance in our society. More than that, we're waging holy war for the eternal lives of millions - and the future of America.

The enemy is doing all he can to separate us from God. He's leading the charge to accept selfishness, apathy, fear, excuses and sin. He's making the church less effective. He's perpetuating the lie that we don't need fathers, we don't need men, we don't need the local Church, and we don't need our Heavenly Father.

In response, we must turn our focus to the catastrophic threat at home – here in our own Jerusalem. That is why we have so boldly named our work The Great American Rescue Mission™.

Let's be smarter about how we approach this critical problem and how we join forces to solve it. As God's Givers, let's not provide just to be generous. Let's invest to impact generations and the whole body of Christ while leveraging impact, expanding scope, and building financial sustainability as we accomplish ministry and change lives.

God created the perfect model.

Over the ministry's first decade, the Lord has blessed the work of Fathers in the Field and provided the courage, the path, and the team to prove that the battle for the hearts of the fatherless can be won. **It is now time to build on these victories and boldly go further.**

Today, He's called you to be God's Givers for "such a time as this."

What an honorable and transforming ministry role! He loves involving us in His Kingdom work, allowing us to see and trust Him in the crusade for righteousness and defense of those closest to His heart: the fatherless.

A High Calling that is Changing Lives and Family Legacies

You will fortify and fuel the battle, where today's Christian warriors change the world for the kingdom of the King.

You will engage and equip the men who are either sitting idle or whose great hearts, faith, and experience aren't effectively put to work by the church.

You will champion and challenge the local church to be the body of Christ. Like Christ, the local church is chartered to give, to love, and to lead on a huge scale.

You will be a practical blessing to others who desperately need help, like single mothers, widows, and the elderly.

And you will directly help communities by impacting the fountain-head of an epidemic problem that commands a lion's share of its resources and social services.

Mostly, as a God's Giver, you get to play an incredibly important part in what the Lord is doing to bring his beloved children home.

Because of your partnership and generosity, we have the profound opportunity to share with a fatherless boy the fact that his Heavenly Father's home has many rooms for His adopted children that He loves so much.

When we give, we follow in Christ's footsteps and live out our faith. *Fathers in the Field* provides Americans a clear understanding of the crisis of fatherlessness and restores and revitalizes the local church as a national unifying force bringing Glory to Jesus.

Please join us in this Great American Rescue Mission™ for Christ!

"Learn to do right; seek justice. Defend the oppressed. Take up the cause of the fatherless; plead the case of the widow." - Isaiah 1:17 (NIV)

The Challenge

FATHERLESSNESS IS THE #1 SOCIETAL ISSUE THREATENING AMERICA TODAY.

50% of America's children – over 25 million kids under 18 years of age – are growing up in homes without their fathers. They live in every community and within reach of every church.

This means that more than 12 million boys are growing up fatherless in our nation – many of them carrying deep, damaging wounds of abandonment that threaten them and society. This is more than just one of many social problems we face. It is an epidemic that is growing exponentially with each generation.

Given this knowledge, our Heavenly Father will not tolerate inaction. We are called to help the fatherless, and now we can.

63% of youth SUICIDES

60% of RAPISTS come from FATHERLESS HOMES

TWICE as likely to DROP OUT of SCHOOL

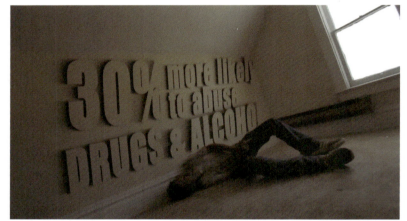

30% more likely to abuse DRUGS & ALCOHOL

85% of YOUTHS in PRIS...

71% of PREGNANT TEENAGERS

The Facts:

CHILDREN FROM FATHERLESS HOMES ARE UNQUESTIONABLY A THREAT TO SOCIETY.

- 72% of adolescent murders are committed by fatherless children

- 85% of rapists with anger problems come from fatherless homes

- 67% of prison inmates come from fatherless homes

- 85% of juveniles in reform institutions are fatherless

- 30% are more likely to abuse drugs and/or alcohol

- Twice as likely to drop out of school

- 11 times more likely to exhibit violent behavior at school

- Dramatically more likely to commit suicide

- More likely to engage in early sexual activity

Angry, lost, wounded and emotionally crippled boys are more dangerous to themselves and others. They carry these wounds forward and fail to develop into the men that God designed. America needs to be a strong and healthy nation.

Generational fatherlessness is eroding the foundation of the family - society's backbone.

(Source: National Center for Fathering; US Department of Health and Human Services; US Justice Department; National Principals Association, US Census Bureau; Justice and Behavior, Vol. 14)

The Central Issue: Healing the Fatherless Wound

The emotional wounds that afflict fatherless boys can be devastating. From abnormal maturation to sociopathy to suicide, boys who have been abandoned by their father and lack solid, Christian male mentoring can develop a seriously warped self-image and worldview. Even worse, the fatherless wound can render the boy incapable of accepting the unconditional love and salvation of the Heavenly Father.

ANGER Emotional fury controls my life. I will never, ever forgive my father.

LONELINESS I feel alone, even when others are around.

MALICE Bad behavior is my way of getting attention since no one really understands my wound.

CONFUSION I am tired and broken by all the different men, dads, and boyfriends in my life.

FEAR I am irrationally afraid. My dad is not home to protect us.

PERFECTION I'm constantly trying to earn my father's attention and approval.

POVERTY My future is bleak because dad left the family and home behind.

PRISON Incarceration may be my future because dad broke his promise and left the home.

INSECURE I can't trust anymore because of too many lies and broken commitments.

DESPAIR I've lost all hope in myself, my family, and that my dad is coming back for me.

When a father abandons his child, a boy naturally says, "I'll never forgive you!"

Our society says, "Forget about him! You don't need a Dad!" But Jesus says, "Forgive him, so that your father in heaven may forgive your sins." (Mark 11:25)

The only way to heal the fatherlessness is through the radical, counter-cultural truth of forgiveness.

America Uniquely Exceptional

Without question, America is **uniquely exceptional**. Our beloved country is one of a kind and we give **all** glory to God Almighty.

Freedom in not man's idea. Bondage is man's idea.

The American ideal of freedom comes only by upholding God's righteous laws, rigorously promoted and defended within the nation's founding documents.

God Almighty is sovereign and worked mightily through His followers in the formation of America. He created a beacon on the hill that has helped spread the Gospel to the isolated, lost, and the oppressed people groups and countries around the world.

When disciples of Christ do not hide their shining light under a bushel of wheat, but rather join together to bring glory to their Creator by honoring and following His decrees in its organizing documents – America cannot help but become a bright beacon for the world that millions will see and become drawn to.

That is why we pause and celebrate her ideals.

"The truth is that the strength of our nation has come out of our communities of faith. Throughout our history, it has been the voices of faith that have driven our nation to a more perfect union." - Mike Pence

AMERICA THE FAITHFUL

What a privilege it is to be part of God's great rescue mission of the lost, and to live in a country where we can openly and freely learn about our Heavenly Father.

Where we can own property and create wealth to spur on and support missions around the world.

Where families can raise children in the admonition of the Lord without hiding in basements.

Where we can assemble in freedom as a church body to worship Jesus in His Truths and in His name.

Where we can proclaim His righteousness and Truths without persecution.

Where we can hold up the Bible as the Holy Word of God in public.

Where we can acknowledge there is no other King but Jesus and not be murdered.

Each of us has much to be grateful for and to remember by giving thanks through our prayers, patriotic celebrations, and anthems.

IS AMERICA UNIQUE?

Other countries *could* also be beacons on a hill, but it would require courage, sacrifice, and resolve by the country's organizers or citizens to follow Him and His wisdom as the defining law of the land. Or, perhaps the Lord intended for America to uniquely occupy this global role.

To date, no other nation is even close in holding up God Almighty in its foundational declarations. Not one other. America stands alone.

Ultimately it is these God-inspired ideals, memorialized in America's defining documents, that make the nation unique and allow it to be exceptional. Our democracy is neither compromised by the rule of the majority mob nor is it an anti-god socialist government ruled by elitists.

Rather, America was forged to be a Constitutional Republic governed by God's laws, where our individual rights are bestowed by the Divine Creator. How we should live, treat our neighbors, uphold justice, and exercise our freedom and individual rights has been prescribed by God - not a sinful man or a government.

As such, these rights cannot also be taken away at the whim of man.

OUR CALL TO DEFEND HER EXCEPTIONALISM

The founding fathers and many others sacrificed their lives, their families, their homes, and their wealth by signing the originating constitutional documents that made clear that the Heavenly Father alone is Creator and all powerful. They affirmed His laws as righteous, proclaiming that America's people are not and will not be subjects to any type of government, tyrant, or king.

It is the obligation of its citizens then and now to defend these precious God-given rights against foreign and domestic threats.

America's citizens, Christians, who do not clearly understand why the nation is uniquely exceptional run the risk of standing idly by while others with a sinister agenda erode America's greatness and attempt to re-write its history. Still others are being blinded or are overlooking the purpose for these blessings – so that we can live fruitfully, faithfully, and share the Good News to the end of the earth.

Much is required of us because of this mighty blessing. Blinded ungratefulness is sin and a scheme of the Evil One.

A MISSION FOR AMERICA

Because of what they uphold, America's ideals are worthy of celebrating, honoring, and protecting as a nation and as citizens – even unto death. Countless men, women, families and neighboring citizens have given the full measure of sacrifice with their lives here and around the world. Many God-honoring missionaries have been raised and supported to give up the comforts of our special freedoms to bring the Good News of the Gospel to distant and oppressed lands.

In order to continue answering God's call to fulfill the purpose of the unique exceptionalism He's granted America, we must boldly and immediately tend to the defense of these ideals.

May we resolve again and acknowledge our special heritage as One Nation Under God and help bring restoration to our besieged freedoms and this shinning beacon on the hill.

Our Great American Rescue Mission is on the frontline of battling for the souls of our country, our families, and our children. May the Lord lead the way as *Fathers in the Field* charges forward for His glory and brings a revival to our land.

Thank you, God Almighty, for your ideals for America, for faithful and courageous souls and for allowing us, in a time as this, to be part of seeing your mission accomplished. May you continue to bless your creation.

CHAPTER TWO

Responding To The Crisis

"DEFEND THE CAUSE OF THE FATHERLESS..."
ISAIAH 1:17

Fathers in the Field is a non-profit, non para-Church ministry that trains and equips the local Church to "Call" and raise godly men to intentionally mentor the fatherless in their own community.

Our **mission** is to rekindle and establish the spirit of boys who have been abandoned by their fathers; mentoring them one-on-one in life skills through outdoor activities, and by sharing a Christian understanding of our Heavenly Father's love and sacrifice.

The **objective** of this **Great American Rescue Mission™** is to heal the deep, anger-filled soul wound that an abandoned boy suffers from and carries with him; thereby stopping the cycle of destruction and fatherlessness.

Through advocacy and becoming a leading voice for the cause of the fatherless in America, *Fathers in the Field* will help ignite a revival of the local church as a cultural change agent in their communities.

Fathers in the Field works to achieve 3 important goals that are biblically founded:

FAITH: Share and demonstrate to boys that they have a Father in heaven who created, loves and cares for them, and will never forsake them. *Joshua 1:5*

FATHERHOOD: Demonstrate fatherly love and commitment to repair broken spirits and prepare the foundation for future fatherhood. *Deuteronomy 6:6-9*

FORGIVENESS: Share the need for boys to forgive the failings of their earthly fathers, as our Heavenly Father forgives His children in Christ. *Mark 11:25*

Combining *Faith, Fatherhood,* and *Forgiveness* with the kind of blood pumping, outdoor fun that no videogame can match, *Fathers in the Field* works through local churches across America.

"Religion that God our Father accepts as pure and faultless is this: to look after the fatherless and widows in their distress..."

- James 1:27 (NIV)

"The single solution for America's #1 societal problem is staring us right in the face, but we've refused to admit it. If together we would have the courageous resolve to restore the family by intentionally rescuing the boys in their distress and shepherd them with the principles of biblical manhood and marriage, our nation will not only survive - but it will thrive once again!" - John Smithbaker

A Powerful Outreach to Fatherless Boys - Working Through the Local Church

ANOINTED PAIRING WITH PROFOUND IMPACT

Spiritually mature men in local churches are empowered and resourced to reach out to fatherless boys in their communities and introduce them to a Father who will never leave or forsake them – God Himself.

TRAINING AND EQUIPPING LOCAL CHURCHES: *Fathers in the Field* is a comprehensive ministry that provides all the instructions, tools and resources churches need to host this vital outreach to fatherless boys in their community. Regional Field Missionaries connect with local churches to provide methodology, materials, training and coaching, and encouragement to engage the church staff and congregation, and to reach out to fatherless boys.

Stakeholders within the ministry and the church partner to be a *Voice for the Fatherless* and advocates for the cause of broken families.

This powerful ministry sparks a grassroots revival of church service to the community. The intentional investment of time with the fatherless boy opens the door to pre-discipling by building a bridge of trust that is developed when they keep their commitments to the wounded and skeptical fatherless boy.

FIELD BUDDIES: Fatherless boys ages 7-17 can participate in *Fathers in the Field*.

MENTOR FATHERS: Men from varied backgrounds and experiences open themselves to be used by the Lord to fill a gap in a boy's life that stunts emotional growth and prevents him from fully experiencing the love, acceptance, and forgiveness of God the Father.

SINGLE MOMS: *Fathers in the Field* reaches fatherless boys through single mothers who want their sons to have a mature Christian male role model. All ministry expense is spared the single mother due to the generosity of God's Givers.

WIDOWS AND ELDERLY: Community service projects are an integral part of the *Fathers in the Field* ministry, giving boys an opportunity to serve widows in the community and in doing so, gain a sense of accomplishment, helpfulness, and self-worth.

CHURCH BODY: Church Champions becomes the liaison between *Fathers in the Field* and the church, working with the Pastor and men's groups to identify Mentor Fathers and make an anointed pairing with fatherless boys. Church Elders and Deacons identify widows and the elderly in the community whom boys can serve as volunteers. Women's groups engage single moms with support. Peers welcome and engage the fatherless boy in youth groups. The family of the fatherless boy and non-churched members of the community are often drawn to the church as a result of the boy's attendance and participation. Church pastors become advocates for the fatherless and broken families, raising awareness and encouraging the church body to support them through prayer, donations, godly witness, and modeling healthy Christian family life.

Redeeming a Broken Heart: Commitments Kept = New Hope

JOURNEY STEP COMMITMENTS

Mentor Fathers and boys meet four times a month, using the tools of the ministry to gain insight and understanding, serve others, worship, and plan a special end of year celebration outdoor activity.

This multi-faceted experience develops a connection between the Mentor *Father and Field* Buddy that builds his self-esteem and confidence, instills hope, and helps overcome the hurt of abandonment by showing him he has value and is worthy of time, attention, and love. Through years of practical service in the field, this proven and effective outreach includes four primary activity endeavors:

JOURNEY TALKS: A monthly hands-on activity, progressively preparing for their special year-end "Adventure Passage" event, while incorporating a Life-Journey curriculum that guides boys into authentic Christian manhood. Meaningful conversations explore God's love and the issue of forgiveness. These conversations often take place in the majestic setting of the great outdoors – God's classroom.

Boys learn from their Mentor Fathers about the liberating love of the Heavenly Father and the healing that comes through the forgiveness of their fathers who abandoned them.

"Nothing invested in a child is ever lost." - Dr. James C. Dobson

CHURCH FAMILY: The Mentor Father commits to pick-up and bring his Field Buddy to Sunday school and church two out of four Sundays. Here the boys foster their church family relationships that provide caring, faith nurturing affirmation and instruction of the Heavenly Father's wisdom and love.

COMMUNITY SERVICE: By helping others in need, such as widows and the elderly, the boy develops a serving attitude and learns that he has value, working each month and building his worth in the process.

ANNUAL "ADVENTURE PASSAGE" EVENT: Boys and Mentor Fathers apply their new knowledge and skills in their own special, multi-day outdoor journey that celebrates their time together and their rite of passage toward authentic manhood. Deep bonding takes root during adventurous activities like camping, hiking, fishing, boating, hunting, backpacking, rock climbing, horse packing, mountain biking, canoeing, and kayaking – utilizing the outdoor passion of the Mentor Father.

"The family is the fortress that God gave us to protect us in a fallen world. When the father leaves the home, the white flag of surrender is raised. The marauding influences of the world swoop in and ravage the family."

— John Smithbaker

CHAPTER THREE

Called For A Time Such As This

FATHERS IN THE FIELD: MINISTRY HISTORY

HISTORY: *Fathers in the Field* was founded in Lander, Wyoming and created by a man who was deserted by his own father at a young age and keenly felt that loss his entire life.

Upon receiving Christ as his Savior in 2002 and being reconciled to his Heavenly Father, John Smithbaker started a salvation journey of understanding, receiving, and most importantly, extending and asking forgiveness.

Smithbaker answered the Lord's call to raise a Voice for the Fatherless and step personally into full-time ministry, leading others to the harvest field of great impact. In 2005 John was inspired to create a way to seek and help others suffering from the pain of a father's abandonment, and *Fathers in the Field* – a natural outgrowth of his faith and love for the outdoors – was born.

To engage more churches and reach many more fatherless boys, today's vocational missionaries along with committed volunteers and a small army of crusading supporters wage battle together in this holy war for the souls of the fatherless.

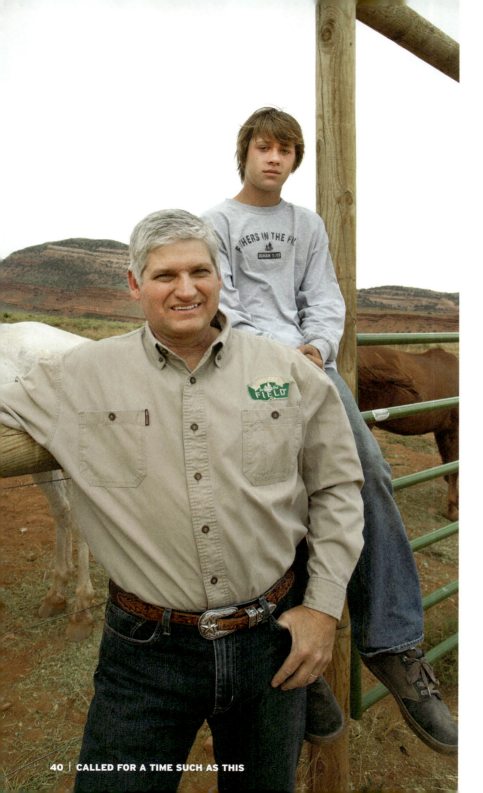

MINISTRY EXPANSION: The cause of the fatherless strikes at the very center of God's heart and He has promised great rewards for those who defend the cause of the fatherless.

Since its inception, through trial and practice, service and the mentoring of fatherless boys, working with hundreds of churches, and speaking about fatherlessness on the national platform, the Lord has extended great blessing to the ministry, allowing it to grow in depth and scope and participation.

The *Fathers in the Field* ministry has developed and refined an entirely unique, efficient, effective, and comprehensive approach and resources that enable the Church Body to accomplish life-altering change for all the stakeholders involved. Missionaries, partners in the church, Mentor Fathers, Field Buddies (fatherless boys), their families and friends, their communities, our nation and the future generations of families are all directly and indirectly impacted by this faithful response to the prevailing social plague of our time.

"We can heal America's broken heart, one fatherless boy at a time."   - John Smithbaker

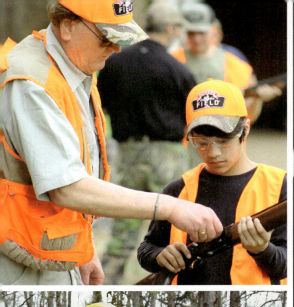

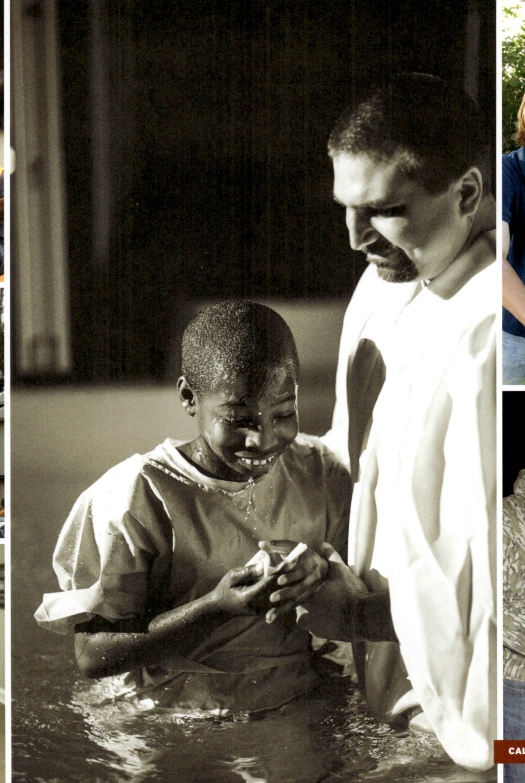

Advocacy - A National Voice for the Fatherless

ADVOCACY: Given the ministry's expansion, the *Fathers in the Field* message has been shared with millions through exceptional national and local media attention.

• Exposure on national broadcasting networks: The Outdoor Channel, Trinity Broadcasting Network, Focus on the Family, Salem Radio Network, Family Talk, USA Radio Network, American Family Radio, Associated Press Radio, United News and Information, and others.

• Coverage in national magazines: Time, New Man, Real Hunting, On Target, Significant Living, Peaks and Plains, World Magazine, and ByFaith.

• National ministry growth and expansion into more than 30 states.

• National recognition and awards affirming the effectiveness of the *Fathers in the Field* mission.

Not only is John Smithbaker the ministry's founder, but he is a living example of overcoming the wounds of fatherlessness through a combination of forgiving his earthly father and acceptance of the grace and love of the Heavenly Father.

Today, John carries the burning torch of truth and conviction to Americans both inside and outside the Church.

Education

Educating the public about the nature of this crisis will begin a conversation that can inspire action and begin a national movement. John and *Fathers in the Field* are stepping up to the next level of activism and faithful service. In the coming years, *Fathers in the Field* will set out to ignite a fire of righteous indignation through advocacy on a national scale for the plight of America's fatherless boys.

Using digital and social communication platforms, the press and major media outlets, partnerships with churches and Christian organizations, and collaborations with compassionate relief organizations, *Fathers in the Field* will increase the awareness of millions of Americans to this fundamental epidemic that erodes national and spiritual health. With its growing family of participants, volunteers, and supporters, the ministry will equip hundreds more churches to become the hands and feet of Jesus for fatherless boys and their broken families.

Fathers in the Field provides an exciting and significant opportunity for supporters and charitable foundations to fuel this critical mission work. Our plan and prayer is to raise and place at least one missionary in every state.

Resources invested wisely to commission missionaries, for ministry operations, to empower and sharpen the church through its community impacting outreach, and to educate, advocate, and motivate a national movement in support of the fatherless.

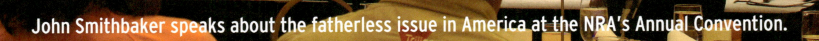

John Smithbaker speaks about the fatherless issue in America at the NRA's Annual Convention.

THE MOST DANGEROUS SOCIETAL ISSUE IN AMERICA IS THE EVER-INCREASING EPIDEMIC OF [FATHERLESS BOYS.]

IF GODLY MEN WON'T INVEST IN THEIR LIVES, [WHO WILL?]

CHAPTER FOUR

Mobilizing The Local Church To Be The Hands And Feet Of Jesus

MISSION HOME FRONT

The missionary field is not only in distant lands, but in our own backyard. Millions of fatherless children are in the reach of every church in America.

Changing the life trajectory - and potentially the eternal perspective - of a single fatherless boy can influence hundreds, perhaps thousands of others in his direct family, contacts, and networks. This impact is multiplied exponentially with each future generation of family.

The following illustration demonstrates how every man, woman, and child who is engaged in the *Fathers in the Field* ministry is an important stakeholder in the ecosystem of God's powerful work with the fatherless. As each one becomes involved in the cause, their impact radiates to extended levels of influence within their family, community, and our country. This is the vision of *Fathers in the Field*. This is how helping thousands of fatherless boys, and someday soon tens of thousands of boys through their local churches, can truly become a platform for change that effects millions of families worldwide.

The Great American Rescue Mission™

Fathers in the Field mobilizes the local church to be the hands and feet of Jesus in an interrelated ecosystem of stakeholders that impact one another and are united in coming alongside the fatherless boy.

Church Leadership
- **Pastors**
- Elders / Deacons
- Church Administration

The Broken Family
- **Fatherless Boy**
  - Single Mother
  - Girls and Siblings
  - Extended Family
- Future Family Generations

Local Church
- **Mentor Fathers**
- Church Champion
- Men's and Women's Groups
- Youth Groups
- Church Body
- Marriage Example

Fathers in the Field
- **Field Missionaries**
  - Ministry Staff
  - Board of Directors
  - Ministry Partners
  - Prayer Warriors

Communities
- **Widows and Elderly**
- Schools
- Social Workers and Law Enforcement
- Awareness and Advocacy

God's Givers

FAITH • FATHERHOOD • FORGIVENESS

FATHERLESS BOY

"We are changing the hearts and lives of fatherless boys, one boy at a time. But we are also aggressively seeking to reverse the devastating trend of fatherlessness in America. Our message to fathers: Stay at home and be the Pastor, the Protector, and the Provider that God calls you to be. And to godly men in our churches: Stand in the gap where fathers have abandoned their posts. Our boys need you to mentor them into godly manhood. If not us, then who?"

– John Smithbaker

1.5 MILLION CHILDREN

Become Fatherless and Wounded EACH YEAR Adding to America's Heartache

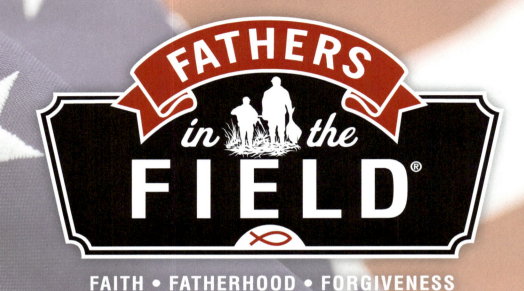

FAITH • FATHERHOOD • FORGIVENESS

Our Reach and Rescue Commission is responding to the fatherless crisis while mobilizing the local church to transform the nation.

In addition to the focused outreach to find, connect with, and pair fatherless boys with faithful volunteer mentor fathers from the local church, *Fathers in the Field* accomplishes **transformational training and support** for those within the local church and the outstanding community.

Our defining values and impact outcomes are seen in **nine core objectives** that drive the ministry's unique, robust, and effective strategy. Each vital ministry component works seamlessly together towards national impact with and through the local church, one fatherless boy at a time.

"A fatherless boy's soul wound is America's soul wound. We must respond now." – John Smithbaker

SENIOR PASTORAL MINISTERING

The critical first step with the local church is to challenge the senior pastor to be a consistent voice and advocate from the pulpit. He must lead on this issue and personally call his men into action to become Church Champions and Mentor Fathers. As trusted counsel to Pastors, *Fathers in the Field* convicts and inspires the pastor to intentionally engage his community on the biblical mandate to defend the fatherless.

LEADERSHIP EQUIPPING + TRAINING

We equip Pastors, Elders, Deacons, and Church Champions with the knowledge, tools, and skills to lead their church body and help the broken family and the fatherless. From the introduction of the ministry through ongoing implementation and expansion, Regional Missionaries train and coach leadership to become the hands and feet of Jesus in their local community.

LOCAL CHURCH MOBILIZATION

We believe in the local church. It can significantly impact the number one societal issue by reaching the fatherless in its community. To do so, the church must be intentional and GO into the local mission field to connect with single mom households - the largest un-churched group in our country. We then unleash the local church's most powerful and underutilized asset, the godly men sitting in our churches, to reach and rescue fatherless boys.

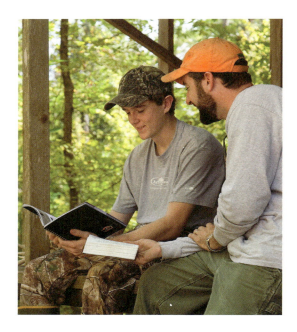

ACTIVATING DISCIPLESHIP

God made men to live with purpose. Men want to join the battle and are praying for an adventurous Kingdom journey. We liberate men in the local church to use their faith, outdoor passion, and life know-how to speak into a hurting boy's life, lay a foundation of healing, and break the cycle of generational fatherlessness.

FATHERLESS EVANGELISM

We translate the Gospel into a fatherless boy language so that he can hear and understand it despite his damaged and festering soul wound. Throughout the intentional commitment of his Mentor Father, the boy will hear that he is made in the image of God and born for a glorious purpose. This begins the process of healing that leads to forgiveness and relationship with the Heavenly Father.

INTENTIONAL MENTORING

The Mentor Father and Field Buddy, along with the support community of the local church, embark on a covenant relationship to address the father wound at the emotional and spiritual level. Over three, single-year celebrated terms, the fatherless boy comes to know he is a priority and receives one-on-one guidance through structured, progressive, and proven curriculum that pierces a hurt and calloused heart.

LOCAL SERVICE

Community service is a strength of the local church. Every month, fatherless boys and their Mentor Fathers partner with church leadership and church body to proactively seek out and meet needs all around them. Fatherless boys gain a great sense of value and self-worth by serving widows, elderly, and others. The soul rejoices when it recognizes it has value through service.

CAUSE ADVOCACY

The local church in America is now in the middle of its most critical mission field. Meanwhile our permissive culture is dismissing the havoc wreaked upon our children by broken families. We educate the church body about the father wound and its devastating consequences on our country, and inspire it be a strong voice for the fatherless, fatherhood, and the broken family.

NATIONAL IMPACT

Nearly every national social crisis can be traced to the broken family. *Fathers in the Field* is a solution to the epidemic that effectively empowers the local church to reach into its community and break the cycle of generational fatherlessness. Listening to the heartbeat of God and obeying His command to defend the fatherless and widow will bring restoration to the broken and is a foundational key in bringing revival to the nation.

"The family can survive without the nation, but the nation cannot survive without the family."

— Pastor Greg Laurie, Harvest America

CHAPTER FIVE

THE BROKEN FAMILY

"Satan knows what he's doing. When he pulls out the man from the home, he's out to break down the family. That's why the man should never leave.

The role of the father is to be a pastor, provider, and a protector. He cannot be replaced and it is difficult to put the family back together once he's gone. Even then, there are always scars.

It is a biblical concept that the family, the community and the nation are destined to pay for the sins of the father. Adam sinned by letting down his responsibility, and the sin has followed through man ever since.

| THE BROKEN FAMILY |

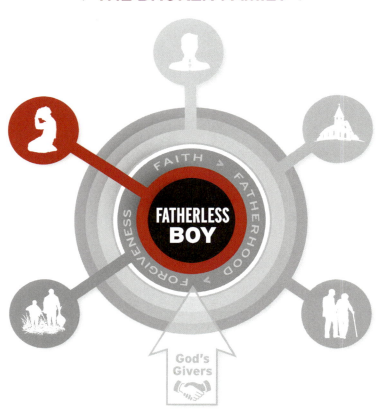

★ ★ ★ ★ ★ ★ ★

Where does the broken family go for help? When the family is the fortress, what happens when the man leaves? Who is the cavalry? It's not the government, not the schools, not the jails. It's the church. The church gets to be the cavalry. The church must lead the search and rescue mission for fatherless boys and broken families in their community. Satan works to cut the spiritual lifeline between the family and the local church. The broken family is surrounded by marauders. They'll get slaughtered when they leave their fort.

The left behind family waves the white flag of surrender when the man leaves. The fortress of the family is the outpost. But the cavalry – the church – can and must go to them.

We are the mission field now. Every fatherless boy is within reach of a local church. We should start in our own Jerusalem. This sets the stage for why we at *Fathers in the Field* take this American epidemic so seriously. The broken family is Mission Home Front."

50%

of this country's children – over 25 million kids under 18 – are growing up in homes without their fathers. They live in every community and within reach of every church. Given this knowledge, our Heavenly Father will not tolerate inaction. We are called to help the fatherless, and now we can.

And, we must.

"I'm not garbage that was thrown away.

I was born for a **glorious purpose.**"

> "The Lord gets His best soldiers out of the highlands of affliction."
>
> —Charles H. Spurgeon

THE FATHERLESS BOY

★ ★ ★ ★ ★

Voice of the Fatherless

BY JOHN SMITHBAKER

"Today's fatherless boys are America's future pastors, providers, protectors.

Men have an ordained purpose. Women suffer when there aren't Godly men. Masculinity is a good thing, and is a great thing when it is Godly. Fatherhood wisdom falls on the shoulders of the men. They are the future warriors of the Kingdom. If boys are destroyed, we've destroyed a nation and the prospect of a spiritual revival in America. Healthy Godly men are needed on the front lines of the Great Commission, but first, they need to be rescued as fatherless boys.

This is why we are so laser focused."

| THE FATHERLESS BOY |

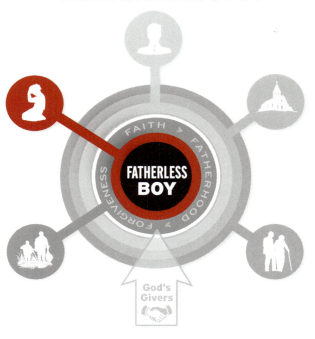

Men without God are barbarians. God is the only one who has elevated the value of women over the course of history, and Godly men must protect them today.

Why is the fatherless boy so damaged?

The father-son relationship is the foundation of this world.   Our God sent His only begotten Son to die on the cross to restore the spiritual lifeline between the Father and His children. When that relationship is broken it creates a deep soul wound. If not healed, it will fester and manifest itself in dangerous and destructive ways. Without a lifeline and a tether of forgiveness and healing, then Satan is having his way.

Laws do not stop evil men, good men stop evil men.

Where are all the good Godly men? Satan is picking them off through fatherlessness.

Jesus gives us a glimpse of how painful it is to be without our father when he was on the cross and He cried out, "Father, Father, why have you forsaken me?"

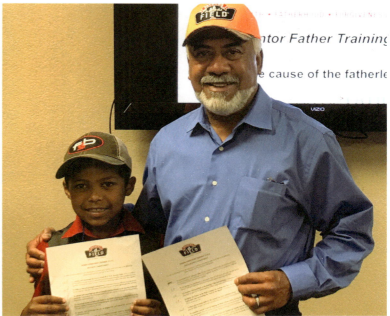

God our Father has given us a great promise when He says, "I will never leave or forsake you." **Forsakenness that these boys feel is a deep, penetrating, seemingly inescapable soul wound.**

We are rescuing the Fatherless by providing freedom from the anger and bitterness of the father wound, of being left behind and forsaken.

Most all fatherless boys believe that their abandonment is their fault, but we talk to the boys frankly and directly about the lies they've been told. We tell them, "What your dad did was terribly wrong and will matter greatly in your life, but by the power of Christ you can be the man you were intended to be. There is nothing wrong with you, you're not a mistake, and you're not the problem. This doesn't mean you won't have scars or walk with an emotional limp, but the wound won't be festering and *will not control your life*."

"When I talk to fatherless boys, their eyes light up because they know I understand their deep soul wound, and because I give them hope for a path to healing."

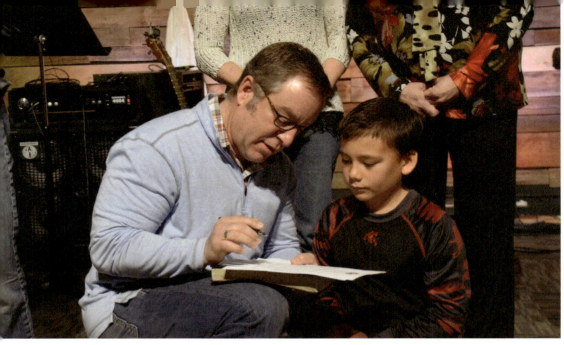

IMPACTING THE FATHERLESS BOY

The fatherless boy learns biblical truths that challenge what the wounds of being abandoned have taught him. Through the intentionality and the commitments made and kept by his Mentor Father and the supporting church, a new narrative can blossom in the boy's life. He is *shown* and not just *told* that he is time-worthy, valuable, capable, important, powerful, special to the Lord and others, and can overcome what has been done to him by no fault of his own.

IMPACTING THE BOY'S FRIENDS AND FAMILY NETWORK

Because of the healing power of the Holy Spirit and the love demonstrated by his Mentor Father and local church, the fatherless boy's life often takes a significant turn that is inspiring to others among his friends and family. It is not uncommon for family members to accompany the boy to church. When the boy's protective walls are broken down and he learns how to forgive his earthly father, the fatherless boy can become the helper to others who suffer from the pain of abandonment and worthlessness.

COMMUNITY IMPACT

Boys who are confident, spiritually-connected and made whole by the love of the Heavenly Father are more empathetic and less troublesome within their communities. Set on a new path of self-worth, they pursue more productive lifestyles. These boys then draw less upon the corrective resources in the community in the form of subsidies, law enforcement, and counseling, and can become contributing members of their community.

GODLY MASCULINITY

The Lord places a special charge of leadership in the lives of men. As the crippling wounds of fatherless boys are addressed in their adolescent years, they become free to develop and grow into their full potential in adulthood. Instead of producing weak and soul-fragmented men, we add to our nation's resource pool of strong spiritual soldiers.

When a father is taken out of the life of a boy at a young age before their masculinity is developed, it throws everything into confusion. Without the resident male figure to imprint lessons of Christian manhood, fatherless boys are raised instead with a largely feminine perspective, which can lead to gender confusion, passivity, and homosexuality.

America desperately needs more leading men who will give sacrificially of themselves for the greater good of our nation and who will share the love of Christ with all God's people. It will take brave and righteous Christian men to raise the future generations who will rescue America from the captivity of Satan's plan.

"Broken boys become broken men."   - John Smithbaker

> "Your success as a family... our success as a society depends not on what happens in the White House, but on what happens inside your house."

> —Barbara Bush, wife to the 41st and mother to the 43rd presidents of the United States of America

THE SINGLE MOTHER

★ ★ ★ ★ ★

Voice of the Fatherless

BY JOHN SMITHBAKER

"Single mothers are on the edge of falling off the cliff while trying to hold their family together. They often make decisions out of desperation and survival that usually add to the problems of the fatherless wound.

THE SINGLE MOTHER

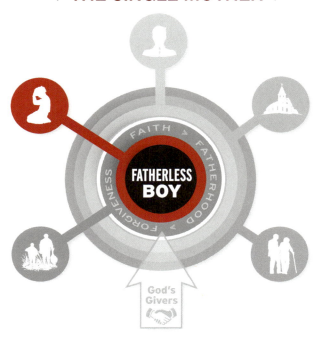

★ ★ ★ ★ ★

Imagine the challenge a woman faces as she sees her boy slipping away. Here's an all-too-common scenario:

After being left by his birth father, the fatherless boy will feel the abandonment issue up to seven more times. He is a frequent witness to ungodly behavior. The single mother desperately and frantically looks for help and answers to the problems her boy faces.

He has no fatherly supervision in the home. He's wrestling with his unguided masculinity. Schools are geared towards female learning styles, and are taking out recess and vocational training. While intact family children go to school to learn, broken family children go to school to be loved.

The single mom desperately needs help and she knows it. She tries in vain to hold at bay a hostile world from her boy. Even if she wanted to ask the local church to be her broken family's lifeline, she's separated from the community as she struggles to work and provide for her broken family. Or she fears the condemnation from her poor life choices.

Too often, we, and the local church, only give single mothers lip service.

Single mothers, the widows of our time, are in distress. As shared in James 1:27, religion that God the Father accepts as pure and faultless is this, "to look after the fatherless and widows in their distress and to keep oneself from being polluted by the world."

A repetitive theme throughout the Bible is that God Himself looks after the needs of the fatherless. The cause of the fatherless strikes at the very center of God's heart and He has promised great rewards for those who defend the cause of the fatherless and widow. Consequently, His harshest judgement is reserved for those who abuse or take advantage of the fatherless, and those who sit idly by or give lip service while watching the abuse take place.

Where does the single mother turn for help? To ungodly governments? To ungodly school systems? To ungodly men?

As the disconnected single mother waves the white flag of surrender, we send the local church on a search and rescue mission to bring hope and the light of Jesus to her and her broken family. What a greater demonstration of Christ's love to a single mother is there than the local church providing her boy help and hope by a godly man and a church family for them all. Intentionally reaching out to single mothers and rescuing her boy is part of breaking the cycle of generational fatherlessness by allowing the light of the gospel to shine in the broken home."

THE MYTH

Mom, dad, teacher, provider, pastor, disciplinarian, and friend; it is simply too much to expect a single mother to be everything that a fatherless boy requires – and these moms know it. Exhaustion and depression can marginalize their ability to fully understand and address the emotional needs of her children. Single mothers attempt to carry the parenting responsibilities in the home that were designed by God to be shared by both the mother and father. Their busy schedule and work load can keep them from connecting with available resources. This isolation contributes to single mothers being one of the largest unchurched segments of society.

However, as a single mother's son is mentored by a Godly man, her load is lightened. She feels more supported by her community and church. Forgiveness of the birth father is a core teaching principle of the *Fathers in the Field* ministry. When her son learns to forgive his father, the single mother is also challenged to forgive him and open her heart to the Heavenly Father's love. Through the keyhole of the fatherless boy, we unlock evangelism opportunities to single mothers and others in the broken family dynamic.

"Every broken home erodes America's greatness."   - John Smithbaker

EMBRACED BY THE CHURCH FAMILY

At the local church, single mothers are embraced by women's groups and faithful brothers and sisters who care about their needs, family challenges, and walk with the Lord. There, they can learn from positive examples of biblical marriages and witness Christian men who value and honor their family responsibilities.

The stability introduced into the fatherless boy's life through the commitments kept by the Mentor Father and the supporting local church impacts the whole family. Friends and family of the single mother who have been relied upon to help "replace" the absent father can also be inspired by the work of the Holy Spirit in the lives of the boy and mother, and be drawn to the love and community of the local church.

Single mothers who are engaged by the ministry outreach of *Fathers in the Field* are often healthier, happier, become less dependent on public assistance, are more discriminating in future relationships, and can be a strong advocate for Christian family living. The beauty of God's love replaces the ashes of her broken relationship. Her personal growth is seen by and taught to her children.

Together with the support of a strengthened single mother, *Fathers in the Field* then launches re-trained young men into the world to work, contribute, and start families of their own with a new understanding and biblical paradigm of the family.

> "The Lord Himself goes before you and will be with you; He will never leave or forsake you. Do not be afraid; do not be discouraged."
>
> —Deuteronomy 31:8 (NIV)

GIRLS AND SIBLINGS

★ ★ ★ ★ ★

Voice of the Fatherless

BY JOHN SMITHBAKER

While girls are also wounded by the absence of their father, *Fathers in the Field* focuses solely on fatherless boys. Sisters and siblings of the fatherless boy can be impacted by seeing the changes in his life and by becoming connected to the local church.

★ ★ ★ ★ ★

GODLY EXAMPLE

The family environment is an ecosystem that thrives and struggles, often simultaneously, in direct proportion to the health of its members.

A fatherless boy who is strengthened and inspired by the relationship with his Mentor Father can become a better brother and a beacon for hope for his sisters and brothers in the home.

Sometimes, the healing of one key element in the family is the tipping point for the entire unit's connection to the Lord. In unchurched families, the boy's involvement with *Fathers in the Field* can be the bridge for the whole family to engage the local church to receive help, guidance, and spiritual coaching.

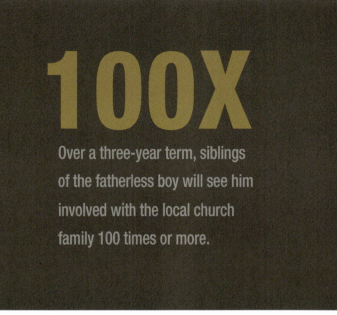

100X

Over a three-year term, siblings of the fatherless boy will see him involved with the local church family 100 times or more.

GROWING UP TOGETHER

Especially in childhood years, siblings have great influence on one another. Fatherless girls and siblings wonder "what's happening" with their brother. It is not uncommon for siblings to seek Godly mentorship when observing the transformation of fatherless boys who are involved in *Fathers in the Field*. Rallied to attend church by the fatherless boy, the siblings can get involved in youth groups and other outreach programs as needed.

By directly reaching and connecting with the fatherless boy, and indirectly with his siblings, we send an exponential number of children into early adulthood with an entirely different perspective on faith and family. The division of our nation is directly influenced by the brokenness of families. Similarly, the restoration and spiritual health of our nation is dependent upon changing the narrative of fatherless boys and their siblings in the broken home.

A healthier family contributes more to its community, becomes less dependent, and is a lower liability for repeating the cycle of broken families.

FATHERS *in the* FIELD

> "Whether America ever reaches its Great Commission potential will depend on turning the tide of fatherlessness in this generation."
>
> —John Smithbaker

FUTURE FAMILIES

★ ★ ★ ★ ★

Voice of the Fatherless

BY JOHN SMITHBAKER

Why is a future family a primary stakeholder in *Fathers in the Field's* ministry?

Because the exploding growth and negative impact of the fatherless pandemic is certain if immediate and radical steps are not taken to address the plight of fatherless boys. *Fathers in the Field* attacks the problem one boy at a time – hundreds, and thousands, and tens of thousands of times over. The math is clear. This problem is not additive, it is exponential. **Fatherless boys leave boys fatherless.**

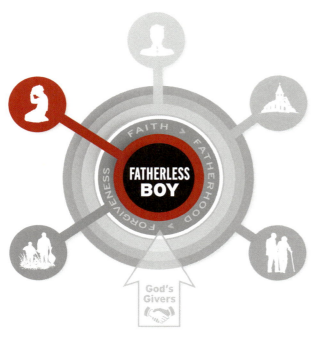

★ ★ ★ ★ ★

THE CYCLE OF FATHERLESSNESS

A boy without a father in the home often does not deeply understand or accept the love of his Heavenly Father. He is denied healthy modeling about how to navigate, grow in relationship, and stay true to the marital covenant.

He doesn't understand that the blessing of children is a sacred, God-given responsibility that includes being the head of household in a two-parent nuclear family. He can be influenced by a culture that has taken a cavalier attitude towards marriage. He may come to believe that marriage is unnecessary or undesirable; something wholly unhinged from fathering children. Therefore, the cycle of fatherlessness continues.

"You shall not afflict any widow or fatherless child. If you afflict them in any way, *and* they cry at all to Me, I will surely hear their cry; and My wrath will become hot, and I will kill you with the sword; your wives shall be widows, and your children fatherless." — Exodus 22:22-24 (NKJV)

NEARING THE TIPPING POINT BOLDLY LEADING THE CHARGE

Future families then carry forward the dysfunctional and broken model, with each generation drifting further away from having first-hand examples of strong biblical marriages and Godly parenting. What comes next? The tipping point for marriage slides downhill when most marriages fail, and eventually most boys will lack their father in the home.

Friends and families will have to scramble to help raise children who lack both parents, diluting their ability to invest time and energy in their own children.

Communities across America are reeling from the impact of broken families today. The lack of stability of the family spreads like a sickness that manifests in a myriad of social ills. Increase in illegal activities, lower high school and college graduation rates, dependence on welfare and government assistance programs, an explosion of sexual and violent crimes, and an erosion of morality and ethical behavior can all be traced to the breakdown of the family. When communities become unsafe, they will be destroyed. Instead of future families being the foundation of healthy communities, they become its undoing.

Ultimately, a thriving nation is simply a connection of successful communities. When future families fail because today's fatherless boys do not learn how to be Godly family men and parents, our nation will surely follow in suit. Historically among the world's most generous and philanthropic nation, America's ability to help others around the world will die out when it must feed a broken family system with its every resource. Therefore, the very potential of future families and America's long-term position of strength is directly connected to the plight of the fatherless today.

"In the 1960's, Daniel Moynihan, and aide to President Lyndon Johnson, warned: 'There is one unmistakable lesson we can learn in American history: a community that allows a large number of young men to grow up in broken families...never acquiring any stable relationship to male authority, that community asks for and gets chaos, crime, violence, unrest, and unrestrained lashing out at the whole social structure.'"   - Daniel Moynihan

★ ★ ★ ★ ★

MATT: A FIELD BUDDY'S STORY

There are so many fatherless boys like me and Balin who need this ministry. Now we need men who will spend the time showing them how to be Christian men.

Have you ever looked forward to spending time with someone, only for them to cancel at the last minute? Matt knows that disappointment better than most, having endured one broken commitment after another as a boy.

Matt grew up in Bozeman, MT in a single-parent home. Matt's mom, Lori, worked hard to provide a loving and stable family life for him. But the reality is, a mother cannot take the place of a father. Over the years, some men tried to stand in the gap for Matt. But the promises they made to take him hunting, or camping or on some other outdoor adventure were never kept. "I figured I would never learn to hunt or have a man in my life who kept his word and would be a good role model for me," says Matt who, like most fatherless boys, felt worthless.

Then Marc Pierce stepped into the picture and Matt's life changed forever. A long-time supporter of and participant in *Fathers in the Field*, Marc made the commitment to serve as Matt's Mentor Father. "For the first time I had someone who wasn't going to ditch me, but a man who was going to put in the time and teach me what it means to be a godly man," remembers Matt who was just starting High School when he became Marc's Field Buddy. Over the course of their three year commitment, Marc taught Matt about his faithful Father in Heaven, modeled godly fatherhood for Matt, and even guided the boy to forgiveness of his earthly dad. Now a 21-year-old college student, Matt can fully appreciate the impact his Mentor Father had in his life. Matt said, "What Marc did was huge. He willingly gave me the bonding time that I needed to have with a Christian man. There are so many fatherless boys like me and Balin who need this ministry. Now we need men who will spend the time showing them how to be Christian men."

While their *Fathers in the Field* journey is complete, Marc and Matt continue their journey in Christ together. In January, the two went duck hunting with Marc's current Field Buddy, Balin. "Seeing the ministry work in the lives of different boys from different backgrounds is truly amazing," says Matt, who is living proof that *Fathers in the Field* transforms lives.

"Half of America's families are only half what God intended." — John Smithbaker

THE BROKEN FAMILY | **FUTURE FAMILIES** 85

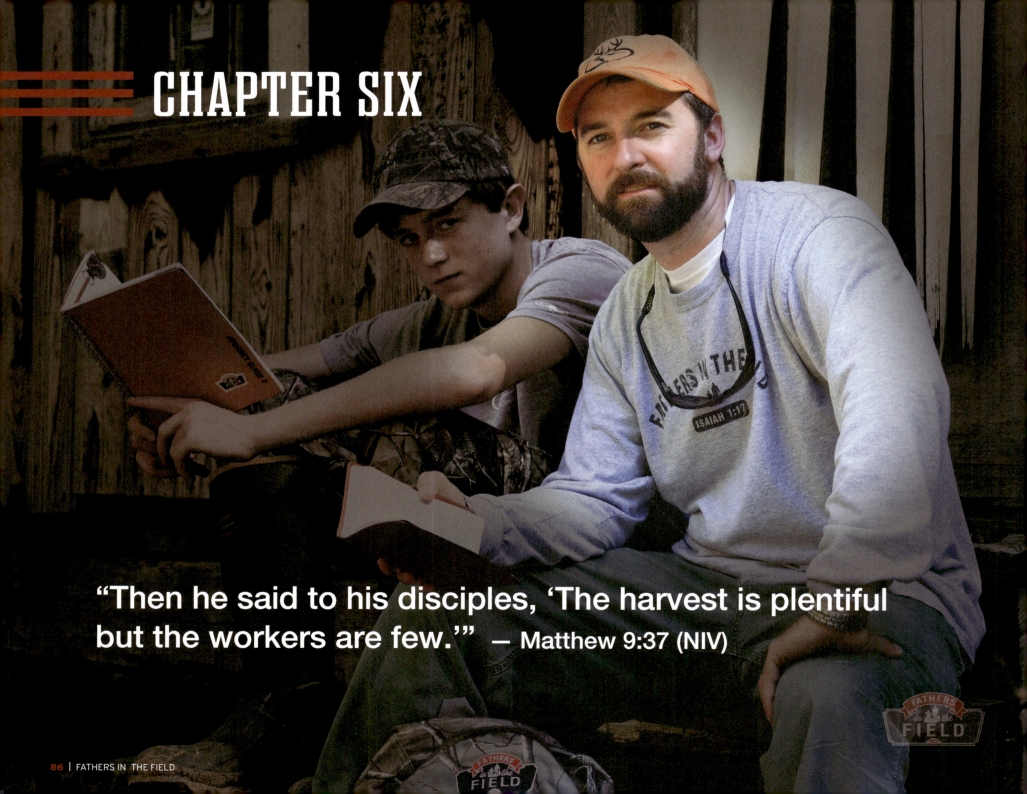

CHAPTER SIX

"Then he said to his disciples, 'The harvest is plentiful but the workers are few.'" — Matthew 9:37 (NIV)

FATHERS IN THE FIELD

★ ★ ★ ★ ★ ★ ★

Throughout history, the faithful few have been called to accomplish incredible, culture-altering change. Such has been the story of America.

By providence, not man's grand plan, our nation was founded on Judeo-Christian principles with a reverence for God the Father, respect for the unalienable rights of all, and has been fueled by the courage and commitment of its faithful people to fight together to defend the vulnerable.

FATHERS IN THE FIELD

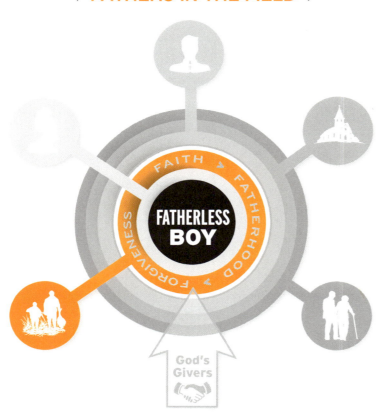

The foundation of our nation's exceptionalism has been its moral compass and its ability to instill values, educate, mentor, and encourage the next generation of leaders.

Two powerful, God-ordained institutions have largely carried the load in sustaining America's greatness – the local church and the family.

Today, both are highly compromised due to church disintegration within their communities and the breakdown of the nuclear family through divorce and fathering out of wedlock.

Fathers in the Field is boldly responding to both of these problems and their devastating symptoms by supporting and helping restore both hurting pillars of God's shining beacon on the hill.

A BIBLICAL MODEL

The underlying key to *Fathers in the Field's* effective national outreach - why we can have success and impact - is that we elevate the biblical model that commands God's church to lead by example, to stand against sin, to uphold truth, and to love and serve one another.

- As such, the ministry team of *Fathers in the Field* is chartered with three main objectives:

- **Coming alongside Pastors and the local church as they champion the cause of the fatherless and rally the resources of their community to directly change the lives of fatherless boys.**

- **Providing and coaching the application of the *Fathers in the Field* ministry curriculum.**

- **Serving as a leading national voice and advocate for the fatherless, the epidemic of the fatherless issue, and broken families in America.**

> "Every Christian is either a missionary or an imposter."
>
> — Charles H. Spurgeon

THE FIELD MISSIONARY

★ ★ ★ ★ ★

Voice of the Fatherless

BY JOHN SMITHBAKER

"Field Missionaries are the tip of the sword."

They are battling in our own mission field in our own country, against an unaware, an ill-equipped or apathetic church to address the #1 cultural issue – fatherlessness.

We send missionaries into the fields of the fatherless. This is a high calling. Their role is to lovingly confront the local pastors, some of whom are the Pharisees and Sadducees of our day, and share the biblical mandate to intentionally defend the cause of the fatherless in their community.

They minister to pastors one-on-one because they have to inspire, or if needed, lead pastors to defend the cause of the fatherless in their own communities. A biblical mandate.

| FATHERS IN THE FIELD |

★ ★ ★ ★ ★

We are living in the mission field where the harvest is great, but the workers are few. **The Field Missionary's role is not a job, it's a calling.**

They are the voice in the wilderness at this point. They depend on God's Givers to remain in ministry full-time to coach pastors, inspire men, to reach those left behind, and the broken families in the local church's community. The spiritual attack on these men and their families once they commit to serve IS real. The earnest support of God's Givers and coverage of prayer warriors provide the needed resources and protection to carry out their sacred and honorable calling.

This is where the hope of healing begins: When a faithful man commits his life to full time ministry and answers God's call on his life by saying 'send me, Lord.'

Their bravery and heart lights a fire of biblical courage to respond to the command of God to defend the cause of the fatherless and widows in their community.

Field Missionaries respond to the cries of the fatherless and pleas of the single mom by mobilizing the local church to restore the spiritual heritage and the God-ordained role of fatherhood in America. Their pivotal role in the Great American Rescue Mission™ has lasting impact on families today and tomorrow.

Single moms and fatherless boys are desperately thankful to know that the cavalry is coming, and someone is battling on their behalf as a Voice for the Fatherless.

They help crack the challenge of the unchurched right in their reach. They breach the door. They break the wall and inspire the church's men to search for fatherless kids in their community as if they were their own.

We'd do it all if it meant only rescuing one boy. But fortunately, men, churches, and God's Givers are responding and that allows us to reach many more. And as we extend the Great American Rescue Mission™ across the country and deploy a Field Missionary in every state, we'll establish lifelines to fatherless boys through their local churches.

SPIRITUAL FIRE STARTERS

Called by the Lord to full-time Kingdom work, Field Missionaries apply their unique relational skills and gifting to engage the local church. Part of that assignment includes challenging the church to fulfill its responsibility as leaders, healers, and proclaimers of the Good News to fatherless boys and their broken families.

Field Missionaries see the Holy Spirit take their effort and use it to transform hearts. They are spiritual fire starters.

A Family Called to Serve

Missionary life is a family affair. The spouses and children of Field Missionaries also connect with the cause and can become ambassadors within their friends and family network. As they 'share' their spouse or dad with the ministry, a family's sacrifice and investment deepens their own faith and dedication to the Great Commission. In an age where "the harvest is plentiful but the workers are few" Matthew 9:37 (NIV), the impact of passing along the heart of ministry service to future generations cannot be understated.

KINGDOM AMBASSADORS

When God's people give their lives to ministry work, they become beacons of the Holy Spirit's light all around them. From direct interaction with the local church body to conversations in the community where they are asked, "what do you do?" Field Missionaries raise awareness of the fatherless challenges among Christians and non-Christians alike wherever they go.

They are ambassadors and a voice of the fatherless who share their critical needs with those who can help.

FROM CHURCH TO COMMUNITY TO NATION

Each Field Missionary may be in contact with as many as 100 churches in their network. By extension, these churches have from dozens to thousands of people in their church body that can be involved in the support of fatherless boys through *Fathers in the Field*. We see a day where dozens, even hundreds of Field Missionaries are reaching out one-by-one to provide every church in America with the opportunity to adopt this effective ministry platform as its own. As demanded in scripture, churches can lead the nation in widespread revival by turning their attention and resources to building the faith of its most vulnerable people.

"We must seek revival of our strength in the Spiritual foundations which are the bedrock of our Republic. Democracy is the outgrowth of the religious conviction of the sacredness of every human life. On the religious side, its highest embodiment is the Bible; on the political side, the Constitution."

— Herbert Hoover 1943

> "if my people, who are called by my name, will humble themselves and pray and seek my face and turn from their wicked ways, then I will hear from heaven, and I will forgive their sin and will heal their land."
>
> — 2 Chronicles 7:14 (NIV)

PRAYER WARRIORS

Voice of the Fatherless

BY JOHN SMITHBAKER

Some people are called to be directly involved in the *Fathers in the Field* outreach through ministry operations and the practical application through the church.

Others draw attention to needs through partnerships and public advocacy. Still others believe in the cause but cannot do either of the above. However, *everyone* can pray - and prayer changes *everything*.

| PRAYER WARRIOR |

★ ★ ★ ★ ★

ONE NATION UNDER GOD

Incredibly, our Heavenly Father invites us to commune with Him directly. He hears us and we hear Him when we reach out through our prayers. Praying for someone or something regularly not only strengthens our commitment to it, but in so doing we solicit the help and intervention of the Holy Spirit.

Fathers in the Field prayer warriors uplift the ministry efforts of everyone involved. We share the issues that are closest to

our hearts and the testimony of the love of Christ with those in our lives.

The local church can take a leading position in rallying a community prayer force that supports fatherless boys' healing, growth of self-esteem, and their identity in Christ.

"If sinners be damned, at least let them leap to Hell over our bodies. If they will perish, let them perish with our arms about their knees. Let no one go there unwarned or unprayed for."

- Charles H. Spurgeon

CALLING A NATION TO PRAYER

Education drives advocacy. Advocacy leads to activism. Activism drives greater participation in activities that can transform communities. One of the strategic roles of *Fathers in the Field's* increased efforts to educate communities is to invite them to pray with us and appeal to the Savior on behalf of His hurting children.

Our great country was established by the unwavering belief of its founders that we are "one nation under God." Intentional and organized prayer has been an important part of everything from forming America's original identity to addressing every major threat to its people's lives since then. **We believe that the wounds and developmental scars borne by generations of fatherless boys are an imminent threat to national health and security. Therefore, we must pray as a nation for faith, families, and for the welfare and salvation of fatherless boys.**

Fathers in the Field rallies prayer warriors at every level of engagement today from the direct participants to local church bodies and extended friends and family networks. Soon, using digital and social platforms as well as the media, we'll coordinate and call to their knees a massive national network of faithful prayer warriors to raise a voice for the fatherless of unprecedented scale.

CHAPTER SEVEN

CHURCH LEADERSHIP

Voice of the Fatherless

BY JOHN SMITHBAKER

For the most part, pastors and churches are not listening to the heartbeat of God because they are failing to respond in a direct and intentional manner to the crisis of the fatherlessness right here at home.

Fathers in the Field is not just a ministry for the church, it is also a ministry to the church.

The Lord's position on the seriousness of developing strong families cannot be understated. Malachi 4:6, 'He will restore the hearts of the fathers to their children and the hearts of the children to *their* fathers, so that I will not come and smite the land with a curse.' This high calling from God for church leadership to support families is not a recommendation, it is a mandate.

| CHURCH LEADERSHIP |

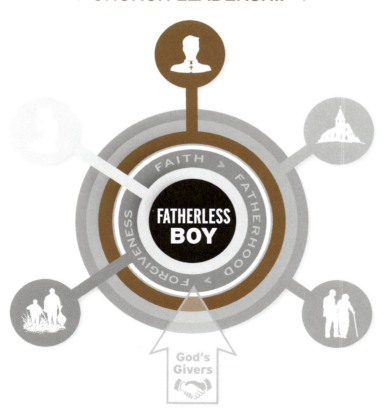

Even before we are able to effectively launch an outreach to fatherless boys we must receive the attention and commitment of church leadership to attack the scourge of the broken family at its key inflection point, the fatherless boy.

Beginning by ministering to the church's leadership, *Fathers in the Field* helps transform the very fabric of the local church to be a powerful and effective cultural change agent addressing Satan's frontal assault on our nation, our communities and our families.

Pastors and church leadership are required to elevate the cause of the fatherless to front and center before the church body as a cultural battle in their communities, in order that the church can fulfill the Lord's command.

"For the Son of Man came to seek and save the lost."
- Luke 19:10 (NIV)

BOLDLY LEADING THE CHARGE

Because we're now living in the mission field, the days of simply writing a check and calling it culturally transformative ministry-while-simultaneously walking over the carnage in our own communities is over. That's why we must first personally convict pastors to be obedient to God's Word. We then confront, challenge, and equip church leadership to make a personal commitment to being a champion for the fatherless and intentionally reach out to the broken families in their community.

The church is being overwhelmed while attempting to respond to the symptoms of the broken family and what happens when a boy doesn't have a Christian father and leader in the home. The pressures and challenges of trying to stem the tidal wave of brokenness in their communities is chasing too many lonely pastors from their post.

Fathers in the Field provides great hope and encouragement for pastors who have struggled to engage their church and empower their men to be the hands and feet of Jesus, the search and rescue party, and the life-saving triage to the family.

In conjunction with the Holy Spirit, we provide the courage and path for the church to be the beacon on the hill once again.

The church is commissioned to GO. *Fathers in the Field* unapologetically, spurs on the local church body to heed God's mandate to "defend the cause of the fatherless." (Hebrew 10:24)

> "There are repercussions to the absence of strong men in boys' lives. Through *Fathers in the Field*, we breathe some life into boys' lives that wouldn't have a chance."
>
> — Pastor Jim Burgen, Flatirons Community Church, Colorado

THE PASTOR

★ ★ ★ ★ ★

Voice of the Fatherless

BY JOHN SMITHBAKER

As the person commissioned with the spiritual care of members of a church, the Pastor performs a vital role for the Kingdom of Christ. *Fathers in the Field* works with the Pastor to establish and execute the ministry outreach at his church with the goal of sharpening the tip of the spear in the battle for the hearts and souls of fatherless boys. But that is just the beginning. Pastors are a primary target of ministry through *Fathers in the Field* as well.

CHURCH LEADERSHIP

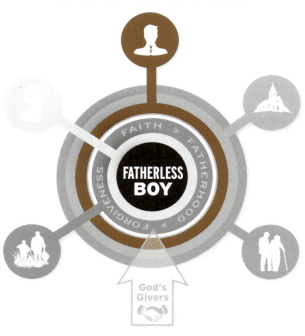

★ ★ ★ ★ ★

It is often said that the local church is the 'hands and feet of Christ.' The church body reaches out, lends a helping hand, and is sent into the community and world with the Good News and good works.

Our ministry *trains* men how to mentor fatherless boys and *equips* the church with materials, coaching and a methodology to carry out this mission.

Fathers in the Field requires that the Pastor make a decision to lead their men and congregation on the fatherless issue.

"So Christ himself gave the apostles, the prophets, the evangelists, the pastors and teachers, to equip his people for works of service, so that the body of Christ may be built up until we all reach unity in the faith and in the knowledge of the Son of God and become mature, attaining to the whole measure of the fullness of Christ."

- Ephesians 4:11-13 (NIV)

SERVING THE SERVANT – LEADING THE LEADER

The Pastor, then, would represent the 'heart of our Lord' in the local church. It is here that significant impact is achieved with the pastor himself. In love and with respect, *Fathers in the Field* challenges the pastor to become better educated to the cause of fatherless boys and the related perils facing our nation.

We come alongside the pastor to lead his flock in developing a committed and practical outreach that his church owns and manages. *Fathers in the Field* will support pastors as they become advocates to speak, teach, and take up the cause of the fatherless. More than a gatekeeper of permission and church resources, the pastor is a primary ministry partner that we will also "never leave, and never forsake."

Most pastors are stretched thin. They are burdened with a multitude of problems, and do not receive enough assistance in serving the church body and community. *Fathers in the Field* understands the weight of leadership and role of mentorship that the pastor occupies. We support the pastor so that he can better personally respond to the biblical call of Isaiah 1:17 and help his church do the same.

GRASSROOTS CHURCH REVIVAL TO RESCUE THE FATHERLESS

Whether leading a small local church or shepherding a larger audience with extended reach due to related media broadcasts, pastors have influence that can spread far beyond the local church's reach. They inspire and teach people that then carry those messages all over the country. Pastors are also very influential to other pastors. They compare notes about how effectively their church is impacting the community.

Pastors work together to coordinate how faithful people in the American Church are approaching both parts to the Great Commission – sharing the Gospel and making disciples here at home, as well as around the world.

We believe that as more pastors catch the vision of *Fathers in the Field* and implement the ministry successfully, others will be motivated to follow and a groundswell of participation will sweep across the nation.

"In America, we believe in the majesty of freedom and the dignity of the individual. We believe in self-government and the rule of law, and we prize the culture that sustains our Liberty - a culture built on strong families, deep faith, and fierce independence. We celebrate our heroes, we treasure our traditions and we love our country."
- Donald Trump

Local church pastors are key to the bold vision of connecting and equipping people of faith across the nation in The Great American Rescue Mission. The next step in breaking the chain of generational fatherlessness is raising up and deploying more Field Missionaries in regional territories to cover the entire country, and engaging pastors of local churches so they may reach and rescue the fatherless boys in their communities.

ELDERS, DEACONS, AND CHURCH ADMINISTRATION

Voice of the Fatherless

BY JOHN SMITHBAKER

The local church is a family and a team. Leadership within the church has an important role in the execution of the *Fathers in the Field* ministry. Not only do they coordinate resources, but they carry forward the heart connection and commitment of the pastor.

Elders, Deacons, and other administrative staff help manage the efforts of the Church Champions, the men's and women's groups, and serve as liaisons with the community to identify service projects and potential participant families.

ELDERS, DEACONS, AND CHURCH ADMINISTRATION

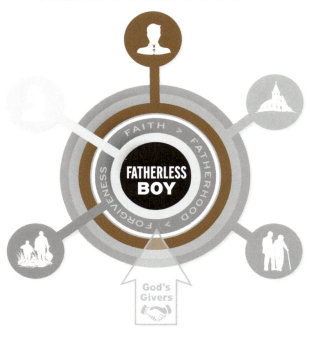

★ ★ ★ ★ ★

A FRONT ROW SEAT TO THE HOLY SPIRIT'S WORK

To effectively launch *Fathers in the Field* at their church, Church Elders and Deacons are educated on the issues surrounding the broken families in their communities. They become connectors with men and women in the church who are available to serve. They get a front row seat to the life-changing work of the Holy Spirit that is accomplished with fatherless boys, and are themselves encouraged and inspired. Friends and family of church leadership also become more aware and sensitive to the needs of broken families and cast a wider net of outreach in the community.

MOBILIZING THE LOCAL CHURCH

Local churches have the challenge and responsibility of shepherding limited resources. By adopting a fully-developed ministry like *Fathers in the Field*, Elders and Deacons secure for the church a practical blueprint for impacting single mothers and fatherless boys. Additionally, they bless widows and the elderly through service projects offered by a Mentor Father and his Field Buddy. **Not only does church leadership then become advocates for fatherless boys, they help promote the importance and purpose of the local church to the community it serves.**

The *Fathers in the Field* ministry trains and equips Elders and Deacons to mobilize the church and the church body to go out into the community and intentionally engage the broken family.

Church Elders and Deacons are part of national networks of Christian leaders who work together to make the Church a more effective entity in bringing our nation's people to the Lord. They help their local church meet basic human needs. They look to use new tools and ministry models as they come available. And, as leaders of the local expression of the body of Christ, church leadership are faced with emerging social trends that threaten to separate us from the Lord and weaken our country. *Fathers in the Field* provides these faithful leaders with an exciting platform to match opportunity with capacity, and need with compassionate service.

"Keep watch over yourselves and all the flock of which the Holy Spirit has made you overseers. Be shepherds of the church of God, which he bought with his own blood." **- Acts 20:28 (NIV)**

CHAPTER EIGHT

Painting by Jerry Antolik

THE LOCAL CHURCH

As Christians become a cultural minority in America, the local church has become isolated, marginalized, and pushed to the fringe of society - outside of the practical reach of its hurting people.

Fathers in the Field wants to see the church battle back to relevance and reclaim its courageous commitment to be the hands and feet of Jesus.

Without an intentional community mission to the hurting within their reach, the church can become a social corporation that is more driven by sustainability than its impact and relevance.

Let us be the church, not just go to church.

| THE LOCAL CHURCH |

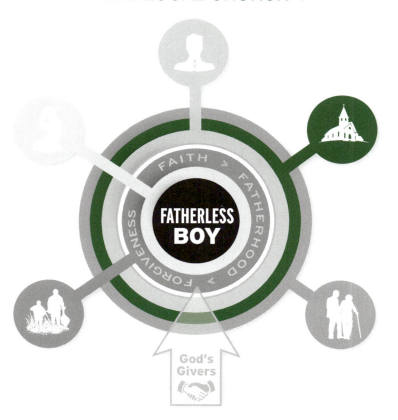

Just to be clear – we believe in the power of the church.

Fathers in the Field intentionally goes *through* the local church, instead of around it like so many other parachurch ministries. As Christ makes beautifully clear, the church is His bride and He died a painful and shameful death to defend her.

As Christ, we see the local church as a shining City on the hill, and have full confidence that with Him leading the way, we can rescue those closest to God's heart, the fatherless.

Where are America's hurting fatherless boys? They are everywhere. But as the great commission says we must go to them and answer their cries.

"As Christ's Church, we must not stand idly by and let Satan destroy the next generation of our boys. And how does a church know - without excuses - if it has a ministry to the fatherless, is if there are abandoned children in their Sunday school and worship service. If there are not, then it does not! "

- Pastor of Founding Church, Covenant Presbyterian Church, Lander, Wyoming
Scott MacNaughton

The fatherlessness condition, that so deeply threatens the very fabric of our society, and our nation's future, is reversible. God's plan, as always, is perfect. *Fathers in the Field*, working through the local church is the answer. **Together, we are the local church.**

As the church body decides how and where it will fulfill God's command to reach the lost and broken, it is important to understand that we must begin at home in our own Jerusalem.

If not the local church then how? If not now, then when? If not us, then who?

We can turn the tide with the Great American Rescue Mission™ - One boy, one broken family, one church, and one community at a time."

★ ★ ★ ★ ★

PROVIDING A NO-EXCUSE SOLUTION FOR MINISTRY TO THE FATHERLESS

Fathers in the Field seeks to reach, connect, empower, and support fatherless boys because they are dysfunctional and not yet reaching their full God-given potential. The same can be said of the Church in America. As a non para-church ministry, our role is to equip the local church to call upon godly men to mentor the fatherless in their own community.

Sadly, local churches are not always the healthiest of organizations. Though full of Christ-following and well-intended people, our sinful nature can sap a church's spiritual power with unbecoming internal politics, struggles over resources, conflicting vision, and theological struggles. These distractions can erode a church's ability to clearly recognize and mobilize to meet the needs of those

within their reach. This is one reason many churches fail to have a specific ministry to the fatherless. Another reason is they lack a clear methodology to recruit, train, and activate Mentor Father volunteers in their church with fatherless boys. By providing a proven ministry and helping the local church to communicate the scope of the needs of the broken family to the church body, *Fathers in the Field* empowers the local church to be more effective and obedient to the Lord's command:

"Learn to do right; seek justice. Defend the oppressed. Take up the cause of the fatherless; plead the case of the widow." Isaiah 1:17 (NIV)

REACHING THE UNCHURCHED IN THEIR COMMUNITY

A primary function of the local church is to impact the whole community - both its members and others.

Fathers in the Field provides the local church a bridge to fatherless boys and broken families who are unchurched and draws them to the sheepfold.

Local churches have tremendous influence on one another and contribute to important movements of the Church. To manage limited resources, local churches often follow one another in who and how they approach service missions, such as sending missionaries overseas to preach the gospel or coordinating with local food banks. All good works, but this approach can meet some ongoing needs and leave important others, such as healing the heart wounds of fatherless boys, underserved or unmet.

Fathers in the Field helps the local church expand its outreach horizon while focusing on a critical need – the broken family – right here at home. That's why we thematically call our ministry Mission Home Front. The local church can lend its voice to the Great American Rescue Mission™ - a national narrative that identifies the Christian mentorship of fatherless boys as being a lynchpin to the health and success of future families and our nation.

> "We need the iron qualities that go with true manhood. We need the positive virtues of resolution, of courage, of indomitable will, of power to do the rough work that must always be done."
>
> — Theodore Roosevelt

MENTOR FATHERS

★ ★ ★ ★ ★

Voice of the Fatherless

BY JOHN SMITHBAKER

"God made men for a glorious purpose."

At their best, they are divinely wired to become pastors, providers, and protectors. But, as our culture continues to marginalize men's impact and redefine manhood itself, the church as a reflection of society, has fallen suit. Part of a Christian man's purpose is to be on the front lines and push back against the culture. But sadly, Christian men are sitting on sidelines of local churches because their God given gifts are not fully valued. Therefore, the greatest under-utilized assets in the local church are men.

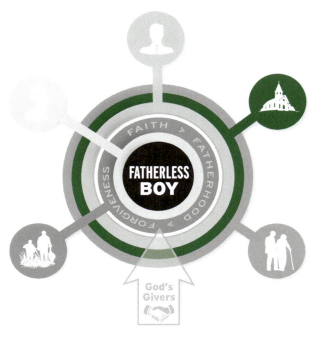

★ ★ ★ ★ ★

By in large, men believe that the church has left them behind.

Churches have become feminized and are unintentionally geared more towards women, having adopted a culture that observes and discusses crises instead of developing a strategy and stepping boldly into action to fix them. Instead, men's ministry in the church can become pep rallies that inspire their hearts but do not connect their hands and feet to meaningful action. Men are relegated to mindless ministries that don't satisfy their masculine aptitudes or they are one of the few theologically trained leaders.

The sad result is that most of the local churches' men are simply disengaged.

"The greatest under-utilized assets in the local church are men." - John Smithbaker

Men are meant for more. Men are the answer.

They have warrior hearts that ache to be deployed to the righteous battlefield to uphold justice and bring help to those in distress. With its men leading the charge, the local church has the opportunity to challenge and charter this powerful asset into meaningful service where the impact is tangible and leverages all of men's unique strengths.

The intentional community outreach that *Fathers in the Field* brings to the local church liberates men to do the work that is closest to God's heart – defending the cause of the fatherless and widow.

When a Mentor Father responds to the pastor's call and is commissioned by the local church, he courageously stands in the gap for the fatherless in their community.

How the Heavenly Father's heart must leap for joy!

★ ★ ★ ★ ★

Becoming a Mentor Father to a fatherless boy is a unique privilege and sacred assignment. Men from varied backgrounds and experiences open themselves to be used by the Lord to fill a gap in a boy's life that stunts emotional growth and prevents him from fully experiencing the love, acceptance, and forgiveness of God the Father.

The fatherless boy is the primary focus of the *Fathers in the Field* ministry. However, through their obedience and faithfulness, the Mentor Father is blessed and impacted nearly as much as the boy. When we give, we receive. When we believe, we can be believed. And, when we serve, we teach others to serve. Putting faith and love into action impacts the Mentor Father deeply. It allows him to share his story and articulate his faith with someone whom the Lord had made a divine connection. Sometimes, the experience of becoming a Mentor Father is also a part of the process of healing from his own past father wounds.

"just as the Son of Man did not come to be served, but to serve, and to give his life as a ransom for many." - Matthew 20:28 (NIV)

IMPACTING MENTOR FATHER'S FRIENDS AND FAMILY NETWORK

Spouses and children of men who pledge to a three-year term of being a Mentor Father are also making a significant commitment to the ministry and are sharing dad with a fatherless boy. They learn about the needs of others, about the core societal problem that challenges stability in our communities, and are directly involved in the *Fathers in the Field* outreach.

Families may have the fatherless boy over to their home for social events and attend church together. The Mentor Father's family gains admiration and respect for him as his compassion for others is not limited to those of blood relationship. Sometimes the fatherless boy and Mentor Father continue their relationship after the ministry term completion, and he becomes an extended family member.

Love in Action.

★ ★ ★ ★ ★

COMMUNITY OUTREACH

Mentor Fathers and their Field Buddies share time together in and outside of church. They share adventure and fellowship out in the field and in the community doing everyday activities, as well as serving the needy and widows through local service projects.

When Mentor Fathers enthusiastically share with others their ministry participation, they're raising awareness of the plights of the fatherless and can inspire others to selflessly serve others.

"When he had finished washing their feet, he put on his clothes and returned to his place. "Do you understand what I have done for you?" he asked them. "You call me 'Teacher' and 'Lord,' and rightly so, for that is what I am. Now that I, your Lord and Teacher, have washed your feet, you also should wash one another's feet. I have set you an example that you should do as I have done for you. Very truly I tell you, no servant is greater than his master, nor is a messenger greater than the one who sent him. Now that you know these things, you will be blessed if you do them." - John 13:12-17 (NIV)

MENTOR FATHERS CAN IMPACT THE NATION

The participation of Mentor Fathers is particularly important because it bucks a disturbing trend.

According to the Bureau of Labor Statistics, volunteering in America is in a ten-year decline, year after year.[1] Some suggest this is attributed to a paradigm shift in people living and "connecting" online. Others reason that insufficient resourcing of the nonprofit sector depletes the capacity to effectively engage volunteers. Another explanation is more convicting: that generation after generation we are seeing less volunteerism because we've failed to teach the next generations to volunteer and we are growing more insular in our worldview.

The church must be an antidote to this moral threat by hosting ministry efforts like *Fathers in the Field* that provide an outlet for volunteerism in the congregation and community.

[1] https://www.bls.gov/news.release/volun.htm

> "Plans fail for lack of counsel,
> but with many advisers they succeed."
>
> — Proverbs 15:22 (NIV)

CHURCH CHAMPIONS

Church Champions are appointed at each church to be a liaison between *Fathers in the Field*, the Field Missionary, the pastor and administrative leadership and various church groups involved in the ministry.

The Church Champions and the Field Missionary work closely as subject matter experts to help the church implement the *Fathers in the Field* ministry.

Their expertise and influence in coordinating church resources is invaluable in assisting the pastor with communications to the church, sharing stories of success and transformation, and working with other groups such as the men's and women's groups and prayer teams.

Church Champions are advocates for the fatherless and can help identify candidate fatherless boys.

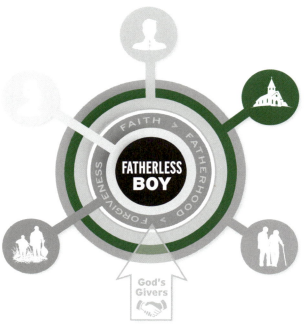

"It is not what we do that matters, but what a sovereign God chooses to do through us. God doesn't want our success; He wants us. He doesn't demand our achievements; He demands our obedience.

The Kingdom of God is a kingdom of paradox, where through the ugly defeat of a cross, a holy God is utterly glorified. Victory comes through defeat; healing through brokenness; finding self through losing self."   - Charles "Chuck" Colson

As with all the stakeholders in the ministry's ecosystem, Church Champions for *Fathers in the Field* become educators for the cause and can fan the flame of interest and support from family and friends.

Running lead on the *Fathers in the Field* ministry at the church, the champion will be positioned to know different people and organized groups within the church community who can contribute to the ministry activities. Additionally, they may coordinate with

outside social and city groups to find boys for mentorship and widows to help with service projects.

Lay leaders are heroes of the local church.

When men and women accept additional roles of service, in addition to their jobs and regular church participation, they reflect the strength of the Church and become the body of Christ. This willingness to meet the needs of the community is what is best about America.

> "The most critical need of the church at this moment is men, bold men, free men. The church must seek, in prayer and much humility, the coming again of men made of the stuff of which prophets and martyrs are made."

> — A.W. Tozer

MEN'S GROUPS

Christian men accept the God-given responsibility as spiritual head of household. They are builders and protectors, warriors and providers. Men are strengthened by fellowship and the encouragement they receive in church, from pastors, and by their brothers in church men's groups.

Naturally, a ministry outreach directed at boys falls under the covering of men's groups, where resources can be raised for support, prayer, volunteerism, and where Mentor Fathers are often selected.

Men's groups thrive when they put faith into action. Because *Fathers in the Field* leverages men's recreational passion for outdoor activities it is a perfect thematic fit. Men who can't serve as Mentor Fathers themselves can instead help identify fatherless boys in the church or community. They can encourage and pray for the Mentor Fathers and Field Buddies. And they can contribute financial resources to underwrite the work of the Field Missionary and *Fathers in the Field* ministry operations.

| MEN'S GROUPS |

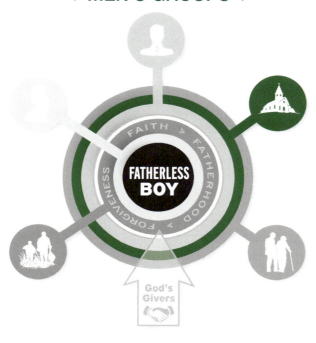

★ ★ ★ ★ ★

Education and advocacy through Men's Groups will be a key strategy for rallying the support and participation of the local church. As men learn more about the devastating effect of broken families, their resolve and accountability to their own family is strengthened. As iron sharpens iron, so too do men in their groups to support one another in their own struggling family and marriage dynamics.

Church Men's Groups can be effective in showing communities what men of faith can accomplish together and as such, be an attractive force for church recruitment.

We need to continue to raise up, train up, and affirm men in leadership roles. Our nation was founded by tough, courageous, capable, generous, and service-minded men of faith.

If America is to return to greatness and restore its spiritual heritage, men in organized church groups need the opportunity to make a difference through ministries like *Fathers in the Field*.

"The wishbone will never replace the backbone."

— Will Henry

"I am not sure exactly what heaven will be like, but I know that when we die and it comes time for God to judge us, he will not ask, 'How many good things have you done in your life?' rather he will ask, 'How much love did you put into what you did?'"

— Mother Theresa

WOMEN'S GROUPS

Women's groups at local churches impact the problem of fatherless boys by engaging single moms.

In addition to being gifted communicators and connectors, women often have access to single mothers and their children both in the congregation and outside the church in the local community. They can reach out to single mothers and help supply the confidence she needs to allow their son to be mentored by a Christian man in the local church. **Women's groups can work with single mothers on their own relationship wounds and assist in getting help for her family.** As women serve, their faith is also amplified.

| WOMEN'S GROUPS |

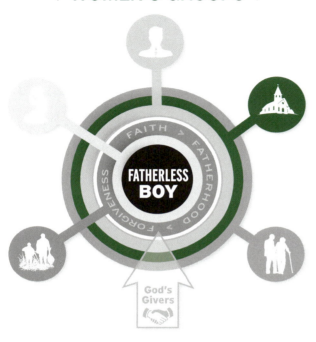

★　★　★　★　★

Men are said to be the spiritual head of household, but women can be the spiritual heart. Moms are incredibly influential to their children's perspectives when it comes to charitable work and giving to others. Wives supporting their husband's participation in ministry work helps to bring unity to the effort and creates a giving culture within the network of friends and family.

Women's church groups often network in the community and are skilled ambassadors for church outreach. They can be effective scouts for single mothers, fatherless sons, and service projects for the elderly and widows.

According to a recent study, there is "evidence that women give more than their male peers at virtually all income levels."[1] In addition to encouraging single mothers, Women's Groups can be powerful voices for the cause of fatherless children, and may be a vital source of financial support of Field Missionaries and the *Fathers in the Field* advocacy efforts through the media in coming years.

[1] https://www.wsj.com/articles/the-gender-gap-in-charitable-giving-1454295689

"By providing a nurturing environment where their children can grow in confidence and character, mothers lay the foundation for the next generation of Americans to realize their full potential."

— George W. Bush

> "Tell me and I forget, teach me and I may remember forever, involve me and I learn."
>
> — Benjamin Franklin

YOUTH GROUPS

With the *Fathers in the Field* ministry, the fatherless boy is brought to church with his Mentor Father and is invited to participate in the church's youth group. The boy may not have acquaintances in the group or be familiar with the teaching, youth group format, or church culture. Youth group leaders are coached on engaging the fatherless boy. Other children in the youth groups must be prepared to welcome and integrate with the new boy.

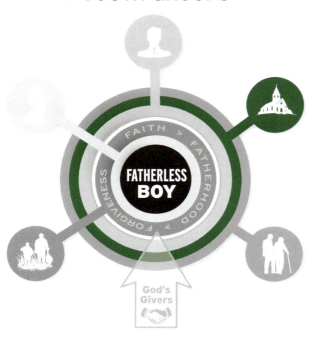

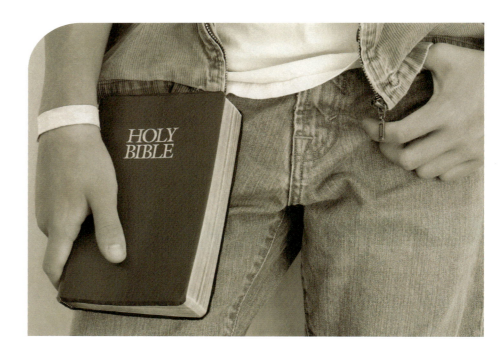

★ ★ ★ ★ ★

Peers are incredibly influential, especially for youth. While the Mentor Father models Christ's love at an adult level, if the fatherless boy also experiences positive reinforcement and fellowship at the peer level he may find the youth group to be an accepting home that he wants to return to.

Church youth groups focus primarily on character development and biblical lifestyle teaching. There, children and teens have a more focused environment to put into practice the lessons they are learning about acceptance, grace, kindness, and serving others.

They can be impacted by their exposure to the fatherless boy's hardships and develop a greater appreciation for their own family. Witnessing the struggles and testimonies of a broken home can make an impression that carries forward to a youth's own future family life.

As young people in church groups learn to meet the needs of their community and each another, they are gaining vital skills that are the building blocks of leadership in the church.

"The Bible is not the light of the world, it is the light of the Church. But the world does not read the Bible, the world reads Christians! "You are the light of the world."

— Charles H. Spurgeon

> "For as the body is one and has many members, but all the members of that one body, being many, are one body, so also is Christ."
>
> — 1 Corinthians 12:12 (NIV)

THE CHURCH BODY

According to Acts 2:42 the church exists to teach biblical doctrine, to provide a place of fellowship for believers, to pray, and to observe the Lord's supper – i.e. remember Christ's death and shed blood on our behalf. In all these functions the church is designed to draw the community together to love one another and love God. **Fathers in the Field provides the church a practical way to make sure it doesn't leave behind one of the largest unchurched groups of their community – single mothers and their fatherless children.**

People often want to help, but they don't know how. They may be generally aware that there's a problem with fatherless boys, but they aren't educated about the full implications that today's broken families have on future generations.

That is why it is so important that the church body get behind a ministry outreach to fatherless boys.

| THE CHURCH BODY |

★ ★ ★ ★ ★

The local church body can join the effort in four keys ways: they can seek out single mothers and fatherless boys in the community and show them kindness and support; they can recruit single mothers with fatherless boys to the church and endorse their participation in the ministry; they can pray for fatherless boys; and they can give financially to support this mission.

Educating the church body about the seriousness of this problem is a vital component of *Fathers in the Field*. Married couples are made more aware of the deep hurt and consequences that divorce and separation cause children. They are inspired to live to a biblical standard and not a cultural or legal standard of the marriage covenant. Couples are challenged to put their children first before their own feelings in the event of a troubled marriage relationship.

Conversely, single parents and fatherless boys can be inspired by the example of solid Christian marriages and families that are thriving God's way. Living examples of solid Christian marriages seen within the church body may have a profound impact in helping to break the cycle of low-commitment marriages and having children out of wedlock.

IGNITING SPIRITUAL REVIVAL IN THE CHURCH BODY

Through *Fathers in the Field*, the local church body can become fully engaged in a Great Commission mission right here at home, where they can know personally those whom they help and be witness to life transformation. In this digital age, awareness generated at the local church level can be spread effectively via social media to and through family, friends, work colleagues and all over the world.

"Church people" used to be an endearing term that presumed many fruits of the Spirit and Christ-like attributes of its members. However, in recent decades the church body has lost some of its altruistic reputation and activism verve. At times, the church body appears more focused on image, comfort, and user experience than on culture impact. Properly educated and equipped with practical ways to onboard support for the ministry, the local

church body can have more impact through ministries like *Fathers in the Field*, and in a single generation reclaim the role of champions of the lost and hurt.

The Lord has used the Church in incredible ways since He sent Jesus to teach us about the limitless love of the Heavenly Father. But the Church can only do what its people will. *Fathers in the Field* is committed to helping the Church be a culture-changing leader once again.

Compassionate service ministry can ignite spiritual revival within the local church, allowing the church body to join the faithful across the nation to address the spreading disease of fatherlessness and broken families.

NATIONAL OUTREACH

★ ★ ★ ★ ★ ★ ★ ★ ★ ★ ★ ★ ★ ★ ★ ★ ★

FIELD BUDDY "Dear *Father in the Field* Guy, "I joyned to learn about God and to become a young man. Mom thot that Fathers in the Feeld would do that so she put us in it. I wanted to be putin it so that's why she did. Thank you for being my mentr father to teech me about God and how to hunt and fish."

Zack, 9 Years Old, Field Buddy, Lander, WY

Zack, Field buddy from Lander, Wyoming

Bill Roady, mentor Father from Astoria, Oregon

MENTOR FATHER "Every time I pick Ezra up he runs up to meet me and has a big smile and is eager to go. You can tell he is just waiting for the next time to get together and do something. Fathers in the Field is as much a blessing to the Mentor Father as it is to the Field Buddy. You see how God can use you to help a boy. And, it's a lot of fun!"

Bill Roady, Mentor Father, Astoria, OR

WIDOW "*Fathers in the Field* has been a wonderful ministry to me. The boys and their Mentor Fathers come and clean out the weeds in my garden, and I can't tell you what a blessing that is to me... I hope they leave feeling accomplished and confident that they have cared about someone else."

Maudie Kenney, Lander, WY

Maudie Kenney, widow from Lander, Wyoming.

Daphne Steed, mother from Brandon, Mississippi

MOTHER "*Fathers in the Field* is probably one of the things that I will always be most grateful for in my life. My son Taylor's Mentor Father, Keith, is teaching Taylor how to be a godly man. Keith is such a precious daddy and wonderful husband in his family. Taylor sees that. Keith is one of those men that you would love for your son to turn into."

Daphne Steed, Brandon, MS

CHURCH CHAMPION "The *Fathers in the Field* ministry is a great organization, giving time to the future leaders of our great nation. When young men are not given a strong Christian male, role model to follow, they will find a poor model to follow. Teaching young men the importance of following Christ and contriuting to the community while enjoying the great outdoors – this is an organization that I am glad to be a part of."

David Neff, Pasco, WA

David Neff, Church Champion in Pasco Washington

BOARD MEMBER "My hope is that within a few years *Fathers in the Field* will be an established ministry in thousands of churches across the country where there are avid outdoorsmen who love the Lord. But whether we're in 1,000 or 10,000 churches, there is no way that it is not going to work and be significant! If we save one boy, then this was worth the journey."

Marc Pierce, Board Member, Belgrade, MT

Marc Pierce, board member from Belgrade, Montana

DONOR "A boy needs a father in his life who not only loves him but also models Christian manhood for him. That's what Dad modeled for me and that's what I now try and model for my kids. That's also why I believe so deeply in *Fathers in the Field* and support the ministry. Mentor Fathers are modeling Christian manhood for fatherless boys. These kids now have men in their lives who are worthy of copying. That's a beautiful gift."

Troy Duble, Donor, Lookout Mt., GA

Troy & Alan Duble, donors from Lookout Mountain, Georgia

Pastor Cesar Chavez, from Deming, New Mexico

PASTOR "Those boys who lack fathers, purpose, and vision for their lives fall into hopelessness and then they make mistakes. My heart is to be part of an effort in our community in which we awaken the hearts of fathers in Deming. That is why I am so excited about *Fathers in the Field*. It is a great way for churches to reach out to fatherless boys in the community."

Pastor Cesar Chavez, Deming, NM

THE GREAT AMERICAN RESCUE MISSION™

FATHERS in the FIELD®

FAITH • FATHERHOOD • FORGIVENESS

CHAPTER NINE

"We must raise up a new generation of strong Christian men to defend the family in America." — John Smithbaker

COMMUNITIES
AND THE NATION

"Liberty must at all hazards be supported. We have a right to it, derived from our Maker. But if we had not, our fathers have earned and bought it for us, at the expense of their ease, their pleasure, and their blood." - John Adams, 1765

"Religion that God our Father accepts as pure and faultless is this: to look after orphans and widows in their distress and to keep oneself from being polluted by the world."

— James 1:27 (NIV)

WIDOWS AND ELDERLY

EXTENDING THE HANDS OF JESUS

Fathers in the Field leads a movement to restore broken hearts and help clear the path for a connection with the Heavenly Father. Acts of service and compassion can be profoundly impacting to those who are hurt and alone. We draw those most vulnerable in our society to the safety of the church's sheepfold, providing education, fellowship, and protection from isolation and the lies of the enemy.

| WIDOWS AND ELDERLY |

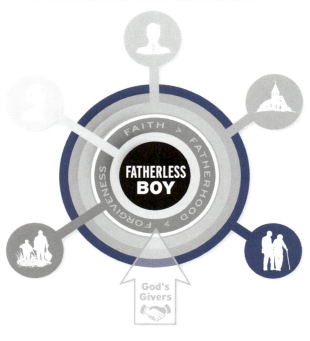

★ ★ ★ ★ ★

Q&A WITH MAUDIE KENNEY
Widow
Lander, WY

What kind of an impact do you see that *Fathers in the Field* has on the boys who are serving you?

"*Fathers in the Field* teaches boys to appreciate people when they are older and to feel good about serving them. I remember this one boy who came one time and just sat beside me and we had the nicest chat. I couldn't believe it! We visited as if we were the same age.

I also know how important it is for a boy's self-confidence to have a caring father in his life. Boys need a male influence—someone who they know is interested in them and cares how they grow up. My sons had that with their dad.

I hurt for these boys that they don't have that and am glad to see their Mentor Fathers working with them. I hope they leave feeling accomplished and confident that they are important and have cared about someone else."

SERVING OTHERS IN NEED

One important part of the *Fathers in the Field* ministry involves fatherless boys doing service projects for widows and the elderly in the community. **By serving others, boys gain self-worth and esteem**. Widows and seniors in the community are contacted by Deacons or Church Elders and can be connected for fellowship and faith with the local church. Special relational bonds can develop.

Fatherless boys are like modern day orphans, absent of their fathers in the home to mentor and build up their faith.

They desperately need the attention and modeling of a Christian man and the support of the local church to navigate perilous cultural times. When they are still young, these boys need to be taught about what it means to be a Christian man, and receive guidance in developing a biblically-based masculine identity that is increasingly absent in the "selfie" generation. Setting out into the community to serve others is a key element in the maturation of fatherless boys.

Communities that take care of their vulnerable are more connected and stronger.

"No matter what storm you face, you need to know God loves you. He has not abandoned you."
- Franklin Graham

"Fatherless children have more trouble academically, scoring poorly on tests of reading, mathematics, and thinking skills; children from father-absent homes are more likely to be truant from school, more likely to be excluded from school, more likely to leave school at age 16, and less likely to attain academic and professional qualifications in adulthood."

— National Center for Fathering

SCHOOLS

Public schools are also in crisis - and they are chartered with educating most of America's children. When families split up, schools become the "catch all" for kids. They are depended upon for thought leadership and guidance far exceeding the boundaries of academia. **Public, secular schools cannot replace what two parents in the home and an involved local church provide for young boys.** Even as greater attention and funds are invested to improve the level of public school scholastic expertise, technology tools, and learning facilities, the problems that kids from broken homes bring with them can seriously threaten the learning environment and is increasingly making American public schools unsafe.

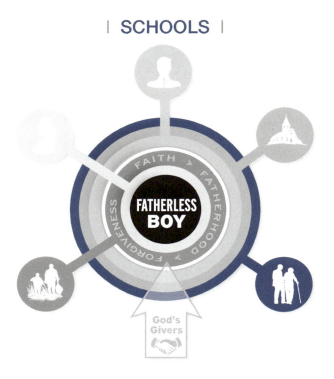

FATERLESS BOY

FAITH > FATHERHOOD > FORGIVENESS

God's Givers

★ ★ ★ ★ ★

Negative social issues are particularly acute for males between 8-18 years old that have no father in the home.

These issues include a dramatic rise in schools of violent and non-violent crimes, bullying, suicides, drug use, sociopathy, and sexual misconduct. All distract from the educational process and command a disproportionate amount of schools' time and resources.

Schools are ill-equipped and insufficiently trained to handle the important roles of educator *and* parent, counselor, pastor, and police. Further, without a Christian father or mentor to guide them, fatherless boys miss morality training in their key adolescent years. The school environment can become a literal breeding ground for another generation of fatherless children.

"As our schools become more feelings centered, risk averse, competition-free, and sedentary, they move further and further from the characteristic sensibilities of boys."

– Christina Hoff Sommers, The War Against Boys: How Misguided Policies are Harming Our Young Men

FATHERLESS

"The most reliable predictor of violent crime within a community is the pervasiveness of fatherless homes."

- Journal in Research in Crime and Delinquency

We must stop relying on schools to do the jobs of both parents and the church. *Fathers in the Field* helps address the issue at the source, one boy at a time.

The church community and a Mentor Father make an intentional commitment to the fatherless boy and become a source of healing and strength for the broken family. The fatherless boy carries his healing into all aspects of his life, especially where most of his waking time is spent – to school. When America's schools can focus more on education and less on the triage of social problems exasperated by broken families, then it can once again become a stronger influence in the development of intelligent and capable young people.

> "If you take away religion – you can't hire enough police."
>
> — Clay Christensen, Harvard professor

SOCIAL WORKERS AND LAW ENFORCEMENT

Fatherlessness is an epidemic in America that has a direct influence on an overwhelming majority of societal problems.

The statistics are irrefutable and chilling. Prisons, hospitals, social services and welfare offices, rehabs, unemployment offices, and the streets are full of men who were abandoned by their earthly father. Increasingly, rehabilitation organizations have not been able to keep up with growing demand. Jails are overflowing, spilling mentally and socially ill boys and men back into society.

ADDRESSING THE SOURCE, NOT JUST THE SYMPTOM OF THE PROBLEM

Welfare systems are overloaded and burdened by adults who are socially or emotionally unable to cope with life, who have failed at home, failed at work, and who are miserable and addicted. Adult dependency on handouts and welfare systems is commonplace. It is even becoming tolerable in our culture for able-bodied adults to intentionally "milk the system," even if that includes dishonesty, cheating, moral compromise, and lawlessness.

SOCIAL WORKERS AND LAW ENFORCEMENT

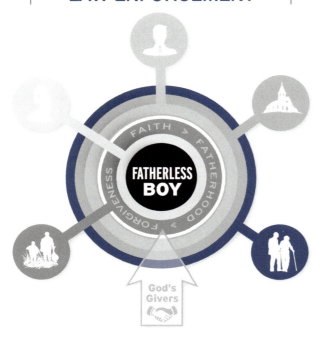

★ ★ ★ ★ ★

THE GENERATIONAL CYCLE OF DESTRUCTION

God ordained the family structure to be the only fortress we have in this fallen world and that is why Satan has so cruelly attacked our families and distorted the roles God gave fathers as the Pastor, Provider and Protector of God's children. Once the father is gone, abandoned boys are left to follow the path of darkness and carry the many deep and soulful wounds around for a life-time, unless godly men stand-up and step-into a boy's life and mentor him in the knowledge of their Heavenly Father's love for them.

FATHERLESSNESS FUELS DEPENDENCE

1. Poverty
Children in father-absent homes are almost four times more likely to be poor.

2. Drug and Alcohol Abuse
There is significantly more drug use among children who do not live with their mother and father.

3. Physical and Emotional Health
Children of single-parent homes are more than twice as likely to commit suicide.

4. Educational Achievement
Children living with their married biological father tested at a significantly higher level than those living with a non-biological father.

5. Crime
Compared to peers in intact families, adolescents in single-parent families and stepfamilies were more likely to engage in delinquency.

6. Sexual Activity and Teen Pregnancy
Adolescents in father-absence homes were more likely to report being sexually active compared to adolescents living with their fathers.

* Source: National Center for Fathering

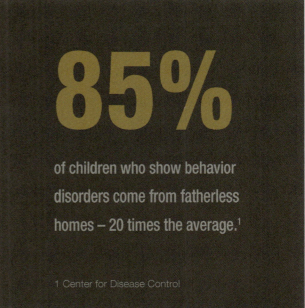

85%

of children who show behavior disorders come from fatherless homes – 20 times the average.[1]

1 Center for Disease Control

Social services and law enforcement are intended to serve the minority issues of society, the aberrant behavior and situations, not to correct a culture-wide moral decline that stems from the breakdown of the family. Our emergency response teams need help! We believe the local church plays a critical role in reaching the overflow that social services and law enforcement will never be able to effectively handle.

We must come alongside social workers, law enforcement, and the federal government to fix some of the escalating problems at the source – the broken hearts of fatherless boys.

Fathers in the Field calls out culture warrior men in churches and points out the front lines in their community. Through the church, it recruits men to start *speaking up* and *acting up* for the next generation of faithful leadership-capable men in America.

The harvest is great, but the workers are few. The Bible tells us we need to start in our own Jerusalem. The home front is our Jerusalem. *Fathers in the Field* is a Mission Home Front outreach. We see our work as being part of a national emergency response team. We must recruit, train and send warrior men – field missionaries to stand in the gap for our boys.

> ## "If we will not be Governed by God, then we will be ruled by Tyrants."
>
> — William Penn

NATIONAL SECURITY

A love for God, others, and a selfless dedication to defend one another has defined every period of security and times of blessing in our nation. In times of peace and in times of war, a strong church has made a strong America.

But America is changing…

The proliferation of wounded boys that grow into compromised men is killing America economically, socially, and spiritually. Men that carry around a lifelong millstone of hurt often draw more from the nation's resources than they contribute. That's an unsustainable system.

Who are America's next generation of defenders learning from? The abandoned class lacks critical mentoring and modeling that imprints character and establishes a connection to the responsibilities of a family, to a job, to communities, to the country, and to the world. New heroes are few today – but "victims" are many.

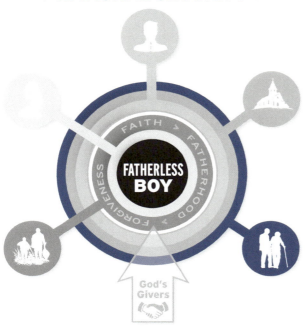

★ ★ ★ ★ ★

A RESCUE MISSION IN AMERICA – FOR AMERICA

Our nation's founding fathers would be shocked with the state of the family and selfishness among its men today. America is losing its soul as boys are left behind by their fathers. Sadly, not enough ministries and Godly men and women are picking up the slack in the local church.

In serious denial, we feign belief that America remains globally dominant both economically and militarily, without looking honestly at the condition of the fragmented family. In our hearts though, we know the truth about America's infrastructure and that our safety is much more fragile.

At *Fathers in the Field* we believe that true security comes only from an authentic and loving relationship with Jesus Christ. As an extension, national security will not come primarily from weapons of warfare and a battle "out there," but instead by equipping the church to call to arms and train up an army of American men "in here" (in the local church). We are ready and capable of introducing fatherless boys to new life security through Christian discipleship.

Together we will strengthen and challenge the Church to be culture changers once again and to lead a renaissance of morality, Christianity, and support for strong families.

"A child's cry touches a father's heart, and our King is the Father of his people. If we can do no more than cry it will bring omnipotence to our aid. A cry is the native language of a spiritually needy soul; it has done with fine phrases and long orations, and it takes to sobs and moans; and so, indeed, it grasps the most potent of all weapons, for heaven always yields to such artillery."

— Charles H. Spurgeon

> "Boys get their FIRST glimpse of their HEAVENLY father by watching their EARTHLY fathers."
>
> — Dennis Rainey

THE FAMILY

UNDER ATTACK

The broken family, the wounded boy, and the next broken family are in a self-feeding and dysfunctional cycle. This may be among the most influential and common denominators that is eroding the family in America.

Under the guise of "equality" for all people and lifestyles, a minority of powerful voices in the culture is deceiving a label-fearing American people. The lie that there is no God-breathed ideal structure for the family is being told so many times that many accept it as truth. At school, on television, and online, children are being fed propaganda that there are no unique gender qualities and roles for men and women.

The faithful, married, heterosexual family image is under all-out assault.

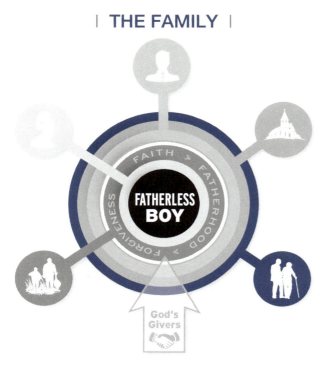

| THE FAMILY |

★ ★ ★ ★ ★

THE FRUITS OF THE CULTURE

A permissive, ego-driven, and selfish social paradigm is being embraced by adults who do not honor the sanctity of their martial vows and responsibilities to their children. These values, taught through parents' actions, convey to kids that their own pleasures are at the center of the universe. Not surprisingly, children repeat what they have seen in the home, and future families are compromised.

However, as Christians we have hope. Everything is possible in Jesus Christ who lives within us. **The same coefficient that produces broken families *from* broken families can work to produce healthy ones if we can break the cycle.**

"If you want to change the world, go home and love your family."   - Mother Teresa

RESTORING GOD'S VISION FOR FAMILIES IN AMERICA

Understanding the problem and the extent to which it potentially impacts the eternity of millions, we are compelled to champion the Great American Rescue Mission™ for broken families through the local church. Helping to heal the father wounds of abandoned fatherless boys is an *impact epicenter*. The fatherless boy's restoration impacts layers of relationships, from his own broken family, to friends and extended family, to communities, to our nation and world, and he is the lynchpin to future families.

With experience and a solid approach in its ministry to fatherless boys, *Fathers in the Field* has become an effective and scalable solution to slowing the collapse of the family in America.

Today, only additional scalable investment stands in the way of leveraging the ministry model and breaking the generational cycle of fatherlessness.

"We are the only country in the world where its founding and organizing documents clearly and plainly pronounce that our, its peoples', unalienable rights are bestowed by the Creator, God Almighty, and not from a Government. All others live under the tyranny of men's rule."

— John Smithbaker

CHAPTER TEN

IN THIS MISSION TOGETHER

We are called to battle for the hearts of the fatherless in communities across America.

It is more vital than ever that we train and equip the local church to become a strong voice for the fatherless right here at home. This cannot be accomplished without the generosity, encouragement, and prayers that support all of those involved in *Fathers in the Field*.

They live in every community and within reach of every church. **It is not just an inner city or distant lands issue anymore. We're living today *in* the mission field**. That is why we accept this great commission and rise to the battle cry of Mission Home Front.

The *Fathers in the Field* ministry provides <u>every one of us</u> the privilege of responding to God's command to defend the cause of the fatherless in a profound way. Financial Supporters, Mentor Fathers, Prayer Warriors, Church Champions, and Advocates for Single Moms all have critical roles in reaching the fatherless through the local church.

All are heroes to the fatherless. And together, we are having an impact!

> "Since it is so likely that children will meet cruel enemies, let them at least have heard of brave knights and heroic courage."
>
> — C.S. Lewis

GOD'S GIVERS

★ ★ ★ ★ ★

Voice of the Fatherless

BY JOHN SMITHBAKER

Fathers in the Field is a 501c3 non-profit ministry that relies upon the generosity of donors to fuel ministry work. Supporters can sponsor a specific Field Missionary as well as contribute to the general operations and cause advocacy work of the ministry.

Being a good steward of the resources entrusted to us by the Lord means empowering kingdom work that is cost efficient and effective. **Fathers in the Field provides the opportunity for Christians to confidently invest where there is demonstrable impact on all the stakeholders that are involved in the ministry's dynamic ecosystem.**

This is an answer to prayer for supporters by allowing them to personally see love in action directly in their own community.

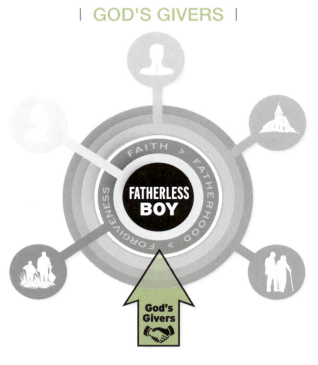

★ ★ ★ ★ ★

RALLYING TO THE CAUSE

In addition to supporting the local church through tithing, many Christians give to other charitable causes. As they do, they become an important part of that organization and the cause takes on special relevance to the donor. They closely follow the outcomes and challenges of the work, and regularly advocate for the mission to friends and family. As iron sharpens iron, donor's endorsement recruits additional support, encouraging others to serve and charitably give.

Thriving communities invest in their health.

Together We Rescue – Together We Rise

God's Givers are then acutely aware of the interconnectedness of its members and will be motivated to courageously step-up to help those who are underprivileged, hurt, or have been left behind. Donors to *Fathers in the Field* have the unique chance to simultaneously support the spreading of the Gospel of Jesus Christ, enhance the effectiveness of the local church in the community, and act as a first responder to the wounds of the next generation of men. Investing in fatherless boys contributes to the future success of families and communities.

THE NATIONAL IMPACT OF GIVING

Americans are a generous people. The United States ranks as a top world philanthropic nation per capita, and are cheerful givers, embracing as a major tenant to "love they neighbor as yourself," Leviticus 19:18 (NIV)

Despite the enemy's work to disrupt and divide us by attacking the family and God's design for biblical marriage and parenting, faithful Americans have shown a dedication to lend a hand and give of their wealth when they understand the *need* and the *scope* of a crisis.

When we give, we follow in Christ's footsteps and live out our faith. Only through selflessness can the nation be transformed. *Fathers in the Field* provides Americans a clear understanding of the crisis of fatherlessness, and to help revitalize the church as a unifying force across the country.

FAITH · FATHERHOOD · FORGIVENESS

FATHERS in the FIELD

FAITH · FATHERHOOD · FORGIVENESS

> FAITH > FATHERHOOD > FORGIVENESS

www.fathersinthefield.com • 307-332-0901

FATHERS in the FIELD

> "If we desire American greatness, the place to begin is the American family."
>
> — John Smithbaker

MOMENTUM MOBILIZATION™

★ ★ ★ ★ ★

Voice of the Fatherless

BY JOHN SMITHBAKER

A UNIQUE AND SUSTAINABLE MINISTRY MODEL

For more than ten years, the Lord has guided the developmental path to great impact with *Fathers in the Field*.

From the lessons learned by engaging hundreds of local churches, pastors, and volunteers to the individual coaching and game plan provided to Mentor Fathers as they intentionally commit to a multi-year relationship with their Field Buddy, to the teaching materials, collateral, and gear that's so important to the restoration, inspiration, and discipleship activities in the field - every part of this robust ministry's outreach has been refined and works well together for maximum efficiency and effectiveness.

Scalability and sustainability are also important when evaluating the potential to maximize impact over time.

★ ★ ★ ★ ★

Another powerful distinctive of *Fathers in the Field* is its gifts multiplication financial model that transcends from a traditional expense-based missionary subsidy to an investment-driven paradigm that achieves individual sustainability and fuels the expansion of The Great American Rescue Mission™.

Fathers in the Field initially invests about $150,000 of God's Givers generous donations to underwrite the first couple years of a full-time Regional Missionary's service, while he develops a financial support network and engages hundreds of local churches to expand the ministry to fatherless boys. As the Regional Missionary's tenure progresses, his support raised will exceed expenses allowing him the privilege and honor of helping raise another Missionary to join this critical battle.

Therefore, God's Givers' early backing of the missionary's

"And the things that thou hast heard of me among many witnesses, the same commit thou to faithful men, who shall be able to teach others also." - 2 Timothy 2:2. (KJV)

formative years is returned to the ministry exponentially over the lifetime of his service, providing critical resources greater than the cost of the missionary's individual efforts for further outreach growth, cause advocacy, and service to broken families in communities across the nation.

Together, with the addition of *each* vocationally-called Regional Missionary to the team, not only do we inspire and equip many more local churches to be the hands and feet of Jesus and bring hope and restoration to fatherless boys in their communities, we also increase the scope, scale, and sustainability in doing so.

Now that's true, biblical stewardship that we call Momentum Mobilization™.

"But the word of God grew and multiplied."   - Acts 12:24 (KJV)

"There's baggage and hurt in all of our stories."

— David McCormick,
Fathers in the Field *alumni and new missionary*

REAL RESTORATION

THE GENERATIONAL GIFT

David McCormick first began his experience with *Fathers in the Field* later than most, at age seventeen. Like so many fatherless boys, his feelings of abandonment and deep father wounds were manifest not only in his broken home, but his broken life.

"I was in a teenage sexual relationship, doing drugs and drinking, and was addicted to pornography. I was seeking love and acceptance anywhere else because of the void of that earlier in life."

"I'd decided that I don't need anyone but myself and my drive. But my drive was powered by my rage and it led me down a path of frustration, depression, and confusion. I was just going with it and it was destroying me. Even my successes were wrongly motivated. I tried to play sports well for the affirmation of the coach. I worked out incessantly and created an image in order to get attention from girls. But ultimately, I was a threat to myself and everyone around me, my friends and my family, promoting bad behavior and taking others down with me."

★ ★ ★ ★ ★

But the Lord, and his single mother had a different idea for David.

"My mother saw the importance of having a Godly influence in my life and got me involved in *Fathers in the Field* through our church. Even though I was older, there was a part of me that recognized the need, despite being rebellious and fighting God."

Paired with Mike, his Mentor Father, David began a three-year process of learning about his Heavenly Father, learning about himself, learning about what it means to be a man and a father, and learning about forgiveness. But healing took time.

"I didn't have very high expectations, initially. I was rebellious, rude, and mean. I had a chip on my shoulder and wasn't going to take anything from anyone. I was so angry and bitter and I didn't take the counsel of Mike. It took a while to trust my mentor father because I felt un-helpable."

Eventually, David's anguish drove him to the hair trigger of suicide. "I just wanted the pain to stop."

63%

of youth suicides are from fatherless homes – 5 times the average!

* US Dept. Of Health/Census

But through their commitment to each other and the process of *Fathers in the Field*, David and Mike stuck it out, together.

"Mike was there for me in good times and bad, and that's why I came to trust him. It's not an easy process, but in order to heal it is what God must do for your life."

"When I was a kid, 'father' to me meant anger; it meant disappointment. But I know what a real father is now and it's because we have a Father God. As I get closer to Him, I'm learning what it means to be a father one day.

Something Mike always told me was that it's not the hand you are dealt, it's how you play your hand that defines who you will become. If you seek God to fulfill you, you'll come up with a flush.

Through my experience with Mike, I've learned how to be a good dad, how to trust, have fellowship, how to communicate without judgement, and about unconditional love. Even now I'm realizing the full impact and importance of the blessing he put on my life."

Even far down the adolescent path of self-destruction, there is hope for the fatherless.

With the patient commitment of his Mentor Father and the effective curriculum of *Fathers in the Field*, the solid mentorship of a Christian man, the love of the Heavenly Father, and the peace that comes through forgiveness - the terminal cycle of anger of this fatherless boy has been broken.

At the end of their three-year ministry journey together, at David's request, Mike had the honor of baptizing him in the cool Colorado river that they first fished together.

"Truly, truly, I say to you, unless one is born again he cannot see the kingdom of God."   - John 3:3 (NASB)

"Now, as a committed believer, I'm changed. Today I'm a threat to Satan and the evil forces of this world that are trying to tear me and other people down. I'm responding to the call to be strong, be committed, and encouraging others in righteousness. I'm fighting the wickedness that's going on around me and standing up for what I believe in.

There are still times when I am afraid, but I can have faith and trust God. It's a never-ending process."

As a young adult, David is now part of a second generation of *Fathers in the Field* missionaries, paying forward the lessons of his new reality by becoming the first ministry alumni to join the cause and serve in kingdom work.

With the support of his mentor father, after successfully completing high school David received intensive missionary training abroad before being commissioned to serve the fatherless in South Africa, ministering to orphans, building orphanages, reaching out to the local community and sharing the love of Jesus to people in a foreign county. Soon he'll be returning to the United States with experience and an expanded worldview that will surely equip him to continue passing along the lessons of self-worth and God's grace that he learned through *Fathers in the Field* to other at-risk fatherless boys.

"It is an honor to share the truth about our Heavenly Father's love and to serve others who are shattered from the devastation of broken families. Here I am, send me Lord."

> "For our struggle is not against flesh and blood, but against the rulers, against the authorities, against the powers of this dark world and against the spiritual forces of evil in the heavenly realms."
>
> — Ephesians 6:12 (NIV)

WHY WE FIGHT FOR AMERICA

★ ★ ★ ★ ★

AMERICA'S IDEALS MUST BE DEFENDED

We are at war. It is time to put on your full armor and prepare for the fight of our lives.

"For our struggle is not against flesh and blood, but against the rulers, against the authorities, against the powers of this dark world and against the spiritual forces of evil in the heavenly realms."
- Ephesians 6:12

Today, our most critical battle is waged from within our own borders. We are engaged in cultural civil war with fellow Americans who aim to unravel our nation's spiritual foundation and make us slaves to man's law; complete with his selfish ideas and idols.

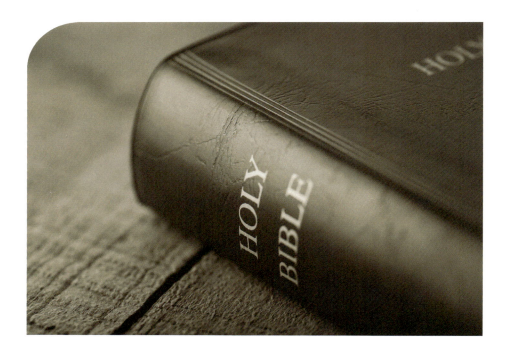

★ ★ ★ ★ ★

THE CULTURAL DEATH SPIRAL IN AMERICA

1962: Supreme Court ruled prayer not allowed in schools: **Destruction of Faith**

1963: Supreme Court ruled Bible reading not allowed in schools: **Destruction of Truth**

1964: LBJ - Great Society Welfare: **Destruction of Dependence in the inner city**

1969: No Fault Divorce: **Destruction of the Family Covenant**

1973: Roe v. Wade: **Destruction of Life**

2015: Supreme Court decision for Same Sex Marriage: **Destruction of Marriage**

2018: Crosses may not be allowed in Arlington Cemetery

Churches and ministries have been targeted by the IRS. Counter-biblical sexual indoctrination is propagandized in public schools. Gender neutral bathrooms in schools… faith speech is labeled hate speech… and our nation's Christian heritage is literally being re-written in textbooks.

What's next?

We Christians must unleash our warrior spirit soon and stand up and fight - or we're going to be sued, taxed, shamed, and culturally chased right out of this Christian nation. To combat this fierce spiritual warfare God's faithful people must lead the charge in the Great American Rescue Mission.

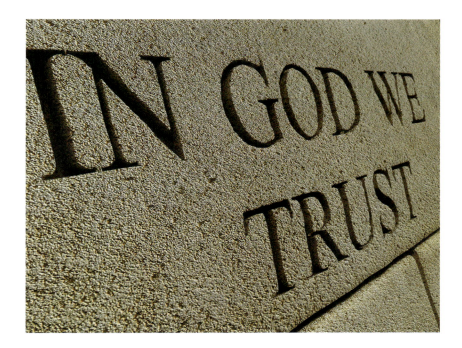

The Heavenly Father granted success to the United States of America so her people could become the beacon of light on the hill - a worldwide reflection of His love and power. We have been given the gift, the opportunity, and the responsibility to share the Gospel while promoting each person's God-given worth and freedoms to distant lands and tribes. However, our ability to live out and proclaim God's vision for all is under fierce attack at home. We now live in the middle of the mission field, battling for the very soul of our nation.

America must be vigorously protected. Our Constitutional Republic stands apart from all others. We have been abundantly blessed to call it home.

We are the only country in world where its founding and organizing documents clearly and plainly pronounce that our, its peoples', unalienable rights are bestowed by the Creator, God Almighty, and not from a Government. All others live under the tyranny of men's rule.

Do not miss this profound declaration!

Our <u>individual rights</u>, our <u>freedom</u>, and our <u>value</u> does not come from sinful men or an institution such as a government. A government can never rule us or lord over us.

"The religion which introduced civil liberty, is the religion of Jesus Christ and his apostles, which enjoins humility, piety and benevolence; which acknowledges in every person a brother, or a sister, and a citizen with equal rights. This is genuine Christianity, and to this we owe our free constitutions of government."

- Noah Webster

As we were prophetically warned millennia ago, the roaring lion comes to steal, kill, and destroy. Truth is being denied. Evil is called good. And God Almighty is being systematically removed from our public squares, our government, and our schools. The enemy roams even within the walls of our most sacred institutions – the church and our homes.

Still, America is one-of-a-kind and special in many ways. It is historically unique and divinely inspired while being heroically crafted by the Founding Fathers. We quickly prospered because we elevated God, and humbly and appropriately lowered ourselves before Him.

The motto of the Thirteen Colonies: E pluribus unum - Out of Many, One

We the People are the rulers as One Nation Under God! We are charged with protecting these God-given liberties. Man cannot make them up, change them, or deny them unless we allow it.

America's Ideals are Exceptional. America's Founding Values are Biblical.

She is worth protecting and defending with all we are created to be, with all we have to give, and with all we have to hope for. Our Founding Fathers put everything at risk – their lives, their families, their property, their wealth and their comfort to forge and elevate these God-given rights to birth a nation founded on biblical truths.

Let it not be on our watch that America's ideals are destroyed from within and thrown into the furnace of history. We dare not leave behind God's great gift of the America He breathed life into.

"The sacred rights of mankind are not to be rummaged for, among old parchments, or musty records. They are written, as with a sun beam, in the whole volume of human nature, by the hand of the Divinity itself; and can never be erased or obscured by mortal power."

- Alexander Hamilton

OUR NATION – OUR BATTLE

Our nation, our home, cannot survive the assault on the family, on masculinity, on marriage and for the souls of our precious children.

Let's "Stand-in-the-Gap", today!

We need to reach and rescue those left behind. Our battle rages on the frontlines of our churches, in our civic squares and in our neighborhoods.   We are commanded to defend those closest to our Heavenly Father's heart – the fatherless.

ENOUGH TALK. IT IS TIME TO PUT ON THE FULL ARMOR OF GOD.

We cannot defeat the enemy with inaction, but only by following the biblical mandate to defend the cause of the fatherless in our communities and throughout our nation.   We know the enemy's plan - to destroy America from within by breaking our future heroes and warriors and cutting off our next generation of godly men.

Given our freedom, the choice is ours.

★ ★ ★ ★ ★

"Who shall separate us from the love of Christ? Shall trouble or hardship or persecution or famine or nakedness or danger or sword? As it is written: "For your sake we face death all day long; we are considered as sheep to be slaughtered."

No, in all these things we are more than conquerors through Him who loved us." Romans 8:35-37

I pray we decide and commit to stand in the gap for the fatherless, the linchpin of our future. The divinely ordered structure of family is our fortress in this great battle and where the Great American Rescue Mission begins.

We are a nation worth defending.

That's why we desperately need the next generation of Pastors, Providers and Protectors to WIN this soul crushing battle for our families, our children and our Country.

THE TIME IS NOW. IF NOT US, WHO? IF NOT NOW, WHEN?

May the Lord lead the way.

I challenge you.

I implore you.

And, I invite you to join me and the American heroes who are giving

their time and their hearts, their financial resources and their prayer, to *Fathers in the Field* as part of their commitment to this Great American Rescue Mission.

Let's charge ahead!"

John Smithbaker
Founding Servant, *Fathers in the Field*

REAL MINISTRY:

REAL REACH

REVIVAL

RESTORATION

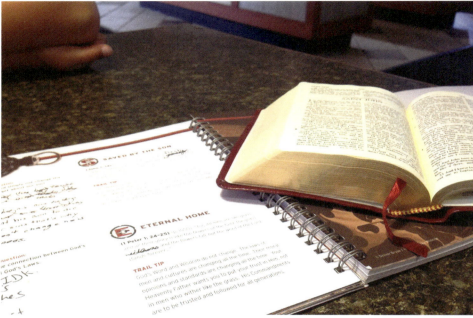

A Three-Year Commitment
A Cycle of Pain Is Broken
A Fatherless Boy Learns to Forgive

★ ★ ★ ★ ★

We have been examining incredible things that God is doing to call together his faithful people to address the #1 societal issue today, fatherlessness, and to fight for the welfare and spiritual health of America's people. I am honored to share the good news of the momentum of *Fathers in the Field* and the opportunity for us to leverage this powerful ministry model to reach and rescue fatherless boys and empower the local church in every state across our nation.

FORGIVENESS IS THE KEY

Before we go out to champion the battle together, I would like to first share one more practical example of how *Fathers in the Field* engages and, in a very personal and specific way, helps lead fatherless boys (and men) to an incredibly important part of their healing process – forgiving their earthy father - so they can fully understand, accept, and embrace the Heavenly Father's love and grace.

First, in the pages that follow you'll read my introduction to the fatherless Field Buddy, presented in the robust Journey Guide curriculum that launches the third year of his *Fathers in the Field* experience with his Mentor Father.

Secondly, I've included the actual letter that I, John Smithbaker, wrote my own father and was a critical part in my own healing process.

I hope it serves as a useful illustration of the depth of the hurt, the deep yearning for healing, and the importance of forgiveness in the process of becoming the person God intended us to be. Perhaps it may even inspire you to write your own letter, should you harbor a soul wound of your own…

Wow...

the 3rd year of the Mentoring Journey is about to start. We are so proud of you. We pray the first two years have opened your heart and mind to a loving and merciful Heavenly Father who cares about you. Maybe you have even given your heart and soul to Him as your Lord and Savior? You are special to Him. He made you in His image and for a wonderful purpose. Never, ever forget this.

This year's Journey Guide curriculum builds upon the past two years and will ask you to prayerfully consider doing something that will be very hard, yet so unbelievable in its effect on your life. You may even think it is impossible.

We are going to explore the most special and supernatural concept that the Heavenly Father shares with us in the Bible – unearned and undeserved Forgiveness.

You may think we do not understand, but we want to assure you that we do. One of the *Forgiveness Letters* that is shared in this Journey Guide is a letter a fatherless boy wrote to his father upon truly forgiving his father, from his heart, for abandoning him and his family. This angry and confused little boy, with the help of the Heavenly Father, found peace and healing through forgiveness.

It took him 40 years to do so, but he is thankful that his Heavenly Father adopted him into His family when the boy surrendered his life to Jesus Christ and let go all of the anger, hated and bitterness towards his earthly father. His life began when he forgave his earthly father.

"You believe at last! Jesus answered. But a time is coming, and has come, when you will be scattered, each to his own home. You will leave me all alone. Yet I am not alone, for my Father is with me.

I have told you these things, so that in me you may have peace. In this world you will have trouble. But take heart! I have overcome the world. "

John 16:31-33

What this boy discovered is that his Heavenly Father always loved and cared for him – that he was never really alone. And, once the anger and bitterness was gone, the Heavenly Father could now guide him into the 'man' God wanted him to be even in this broken world. Out of bad and hard situations, Good things can come out of those bad and hard experiences.

Situations will never be perfect until we are home with our Heavenly Father, but with the help and guidance of the Holy Spirit in our lives, we can accomplish great and mighty things on our Heavenly Father's behalf. We understand, it may take some time before you are actually ready to write this *Forgiveness Letter*.

But, also know, this letter will need to be written if you truly want to understand God's plan for your life and become the man your Heavenly Father has planned for you. There is no way around forgiveness.

4

Thank you for taking this **Forgiveness Journey** with us and with your Mentor Father. We earnestly pray that you seek your Heavenly Father and that you call on His precious Son's name, Jesus, in faith, for your eternal salvation.

Be assured that if you call on His name to rescue you from this broken world, repent of your sins and ask for forgiveness, He will surely hear you calling His name. And He will answer!

The Heavenly Father's house has many rooms. He will love you and never leave nor forsake you. That is a promise and a commitment you can count on!

Be God's man.

With Love and Understanding, *Fathers in the Field* Ministry and a fatherless boy who knows your pain.

John Smithbaker
Founding Servant

JOURNEY TEAM

Your Name

_____

Mentor Father Name

_____

Celebration Event

_____

_____

> ## Journey Path:

MONTH 1: 6	**MONTH 5:** 46	**MONTH 9:** 86
MONTH 2: 16	**MONTH 6:** 56	**MONTH 10:** 96
MONTH 3: 26	**MONTH 7:** 66	**THOUGHTS:** 106
MONTH 4: 36	**MONTH 8:** 76	**LETTER:** 107

Ministry printing costs were in part graciously underwritten through the generousity of:

> **The Hodgdon Family Fund**
> **Richardson Family Foundation**
> **Scott Schultz, Scent Blocker**
> **Neiman Enterprises, Inc.**
> **Larry and Brenda Potterfield**

FATHERS IN THE FIELD ➤ *5* ➤

March 2003

Dear Dad,

I write this letter in sincere trepidation, but relieved sorrow. I have been living with the deepest pain, anger and disappointment over your abandonment of Kym and me—I was just born and Kym was three years old. I will be forty this October.

I write this letter to wash clean my wound that I did not know how to heal until now. I want you to know that I entered this life and grew up without a father to hold me, protect me, guide me into manhood or to sacrifice for me. Instead, you gave your son up for some other convenient life. Your love and time went to others for which you gave up as well. Therefore, so you understand completely, you abandoned Kym and me for something you threw away. Again, you abandoned Kym and me for something you threw away. Those are powerful actions with a profound meaning to living souls. Deep wounds that you created that I am now able to heal. However, I now realize I will never have that opportunity with you, time has gone by. This is painful to write, but so necessary. As I unburden and heal my soul, I do want you to know where I am coming from and the purpose of this letter. I want you to know, that what you did was terribly wrong, it mattered greatly in my life, and that I have come to forgive you.

As I hold my son and daughters, I could not even imagine turning them over to the world without me there. I did not understand fully why this deep wound and hurt would not heal. My anger has grown inside me as I see me in my son. The scabs have finally been torn off for the last time. As I catch my children in my arms as I arrive home from work, as I read to my children, comfort them during periods of pain, experience their daily achievements, participate in their memories, and to honestly, completely be there for them as a father is called to do, I understand where my anger and hurt is coming from. I have said I love you all my life as something I was supposed to do, out of respect. It was not a love I now know should have existed. I bristle every time you say I acted a certain way as a baby when you referring to my John Spencer. You were not there. You would not know. I do not have childhood memories, stories or traditions to share about my father with my children. But rather, I have confusion and questions I can not answer to myself or family. Not once have you ever explained, shown remorse, regret, or discussed your actions. Kym and I have done all of the sacrificing for you and on your behalf. I thank the Lord and Savoir for the angels he sent to watch over me. They have always been there and I give thanks every night. I thank my mom for being such a strong person and caring mother. My love for her could not be any stronger. She gave unconditionally and sacrificed totally of herself for her children. I saw her joy and love for us through all her unselfish pain and loneliness as she made decisions out of necessity. I saw my big sister starve for love for a father that was not there for her. Her search took painful directions. I am so proud of her for being so strong and becoming such a loving person. I love my memories of my Uncle Bucky. He was the man of my life growing up. I learned from him as I grew up in search of what it meant to be a man. I learned to be fun from him. He took the time to be our Santa Claus. I felt the joy of throwing a baseball as high as I could to him and felt the thrill of catching the baseball that touched the stars from him. He gave me confidence and I will forever be grateful to him. Where were you? Devoting all your time and energy to others and not your children—only to lose it all. I do not understand.

Your efforts toward me as I was older have been noticed, but I have been unable to fully accept or appreciate them. I now know why. There is no foundation to build on. I would, however, like to share with you a moment I cherish deeply. A son needs to know his name—who he is in this world. Upon me entering high school, you made it clear to me you wanted me to use my birth name—Smithbaker. You gave me the courage to fight for that name and I got it changed my freshman year. I remember saying to myself, I now, at least know my name – I know who I am. As symbolic as it may sound, it meant everything to me at that time. And, it still does.

I cry as I write this, tears of yesterday's pain and tears of wounds healed. I have a selfish prayer... I pray for your soul that you may find our Lord, Jesus so that we will not be separated again upon departure from this earth. Father and son are meant to be together. It is a gift from God that should not be thrown away.

Thank you for reading this and I truly hope you understand my purpose. It is my prayer that in the time remaining, we can have a relationship that deepens.

Your son, John Joseph Smithbaker, III

ABOUT THE AUTHOR

"We are introducing abandoned boys to the true hope that comes only through Christ, in a Father/Son experience adventuring in God's great outdoors."

The first four decades of John's storyline reads like most men's. He fought hard in his quest for peace and contentment through success, financial gain and accomplishments. And, like many people today, he came from a broken home. There was a break in the cup. It didn't matter how hard and fast John tried to fill it up.

He built a distinguished career as CEO of Brunton Group, a leading manufacturer of outdoor adventure products. During his 15-year tenure, John adeptly led the expansion of the Wyoming-based company, received accolades for bringing jobs back to Wyoming from overseas and garnered awards for his leadership and innovative product development.

As an avid outdoorsman working in the industry, it was a perfect intersect of John's passions and pursuits. Although he held the reigns of an international conglomerate, but couldn't get a grip on his insatiable longing to reconcile the pain, rejection and lack of approval from a father that deserted his family.

John endlessly struggled to make sense of his father choosing to leave the family when his mom was pregnant with him and his older sister who was three-years- old at the time. The consequences of his father giving up his role as pastor, provider and protector of the family wreaked havoc in John's boyhood and manhood. Outwardly, his success was envious, but inwardly, his struggles were not. He desperately wanted to leave the bitterness and anger behind and learn to forgive. It took until his 40th year.

That milestone year, John stopped chasing temporal things and embraced God's eternal truth about love and forgiveness for the first time. While driving a dark, dirt road near his home in Lander, WY in 2002, John cried out to God. Over time and by God's grace, John began to heal from deep wounds inflicted by his father's absence. Exhaustion and frustration gave way to fulfillment and the assurance of God the Father's abiding love.

In 2005, John launched **Fathers in the Field** to share God's love with hurting boys dealing with the same abandonment issues he dealt with for so long. His goal is to help prevent the devastating cycle of earthy father abandonment before these boys become men by sharing their Heavenly Father's staying power, forgiveness and faithfulness.

Seven years of balancing CEO and the growing demands of a national ministry, God began to prompt John to lean into Him and submit to His calling. After some spiritual wrestling matches with God, John joyously surrendered knowing he was doing the right thing for all the right reasons. In the fall of 2012, John resigned from Brunton Outdoor to focus full-time on *Fathers in the Field's* outreach to some of the 13 million fatherless boys in the United States.

Since then, Smithbaker has become an author, speaker, mentor, major media resource, and a trusted advisor to pastors and Christian leaders across the country. The Lord is using his story and committed resolve as a national voice for the fatherless to launch this Great American Rescue Mission. These focused efforts address the #1 societal issue in our nation, ignite a spiritual revival in and through the local church, and will end the generational cycle of fatherlessness through the *Fathers in the Field* ministry.

John's desire is to be a catalyst for the Kingdom by "defending the cause of the fatherless." He knows he cannot be compassionate from a distance. John's all in, his sleeves rolled up and working in the field across America, encouraging the church and men to make a stand for the fatherless in their community.

Join us in The Great American Rescue Mission!

CONTACT
Fathers in the Field

PHONE
1-844-ISAIAH-1 (1-844-472-4241)

EMAIL
info@fathersinthefield.com

★ ★ ★ ★ ★ ★ ★ ★ ★ ★

THANK YOU

CPSIA information can be obtained at www.ICGtesting.com
Printed in the USA
LVIW012109210319
611395LV00001B/1

*9 7 8 1 9 4 2 4 6 4 6 4 8 *